NEVER
TURNING
BACK

The Well-Walked Life of
Sally Alice Thompson

by

Nancy Warnock Harmon

ISBN 978-1-943841-20-2

Back cover graphic by Freepik
Book design by J.K. McGann

Printed in the United States of America
Albuquerque, New Mexico, USA

This book is dedicated to those who believe our world can be more peaceful, equitable, and just, and who are working together to create that reality. A special thanks to those who have given generously of their time and resources to sustain the work of the Albuquerque Center for Peace and Justice.

Acknowledgments

Although this is a very short book, it has taken the help of many people to produce it. First, thanks to Caroline Monie and the late Betsy Morrison for beginning this project and allowing me to join in. Thanks to the many friends and colleagues of Sally Alice for hours of fun and fascinating interviews. I have learned a lot not only about Sally Alice but also about each of you and the important work that brought you together with her. Your dedication and tenacity give me hope. Special thanks to those who read the manuscript and added insights and encouragement: my sister Judy, a careful reader and an honest critic; my friend Beverly who caught errors as she listened because she's blind; my friend and colleague Denise, whose writing I admire greatly; my friend Mary, another tireless activist for peace; and friends Iris and Sharon, both writer friends who have shared their own writing experience to keep me motivated. I am grateful to you all.

The title of this book comes from a song written by Pat Humphries and performed by Pat and Sandy O of the band Emma's Revolution. Pat and Sandy exchanged songs with Sally Alice one afternoon in 2017 when they performed in Albuquerque.

Never Turning Back

We're gonna keep on walking forward
Keep on walking forward, keep on walking forward
Never turning back, never turning back

We're gonna keep on singing loudly
Keep on singing loudly, keep on singing loudly
Never turning back, never turning back

We're gonna keep on loving boldly
Keep on loving boldly, keep on loving boldly
Never turning back, never turning back

We're gonna work for change together
Work for change together, work for change together
Never turning back, never turning back

We're gonna reach across our borders
Reach across our borders, reach across our borders
Never turning back, never turning back

We're gonna keep on walking forward
Keep on walking forward, keep on walking forward
Never turning back, never turning back

Music and words by Pat Humphries (1984)
© Pat Humphries 1984; Big Sing Community 2019

Preface

April 1986

The roar of a helicopter ripped the air as it hovered, stirring up clouds of dust. An eager crowd of 2,000 people, waiting anxiously to meet the organizer of the Great Peace March of 1986, watched as it descended. They were eager to begin the march and needed their final instructions. Instead, a voice boomed from above, announcing, "We have lost our sponsor and we are bankrupt. Go home; the march is canceled. Go home now; there is no more march!" After repeating the announcement several times, the voice and the 'copter ascended into the gathering rain clouds and disappeared.

People looked at each other in disbelief. How could this be? Just days ago, Holly Near had sent them off from Los Angeles in a burst of song, and they had already walked 114 miles to Barstow in the California desert. After planning for months, bringing tents and supplies, children and dogs, they were supposed to go home?

As wind began to drive rain against the tents, some of the less committed marchers decided to do just that. More than half of them packed up and left, but the others, too dazed or angry or disappointed to make a quick decision, lingered on. Among them was Sally Alice Thompson, 63 years old and a committed peace and justice activist from Albuquerque,

New Mexico. She'd come this far and was determined not to give up.

Sure enough, as the rain and people's minds cleared the next day, there was talk of regrouping and continuing. Talk turned into heated discussion about strategy and logistics, which, in a few more days, turned into frenzied action. Leaders emerged and people volunteered for various tasks—teachers for kids on the march, cooks for the kitchen truck, and Portapotty Bob to maintain the camp's sanitation and health. The march finally took off with the marchers in high spirits after two weeks of organizing. Eight and a half months and over 3,000 miles later, Sally Alice and 800 others reached Washington DC.

August 2023

There's much more to the story of the march, and to the story of Sally Alice—an icon of the social justice community in Albuquerque, New Mexico, who has worked tirelessly on issues of peace and justice with the same determination and commitment she showed in 1986. It's been a lifelong effort, and by coupling that commitment with compassion and generosity, she has made a lasting impact on the peace and justice movement locally, nationally, and internationally. If she's been discouraged, she doesn't show that face publicly. Today at 99, she remains humble and self-effacing, insisting her story is not worth telling, but many of us who know her think that it is.

I first met Sally Alice in the mid 1990s, when the US had imposed sanctions on the Saddam Hussein regime in Iraq, and the Iraqi people, including millions of children, were starving. A group gathered regularly at the Albuquerque Center for Peace and Justice to create flyers and plan demonstrations. In the 1980s, Sally Alice had been one of the founding mothers of the Peace Center, which started in one room to support an international movement calling for a ban on the proliferation of nuclear weapons. Through the work of many people, it expanded into an umbrella organization of more than 70 social justice organizations.

Over the many decades of her activism, Sally Alice also created a Sister Cities program between Ashgabat, Turkmenistan (which she visited 29 times) and Albuquerque, organized a local Veterans For Peace chapter, and wrote irreverent lyrics for Raging Grannies songs. She has walked to Santa Fe to protest the influence of money in our political system and walked her talk by opening her home to those fleeing violence. She has written two books from unique perspectives, one about her experiences in Turkmenistan, *Central Asia Fantasia*, and a novel about a pioneer woman adopted by an Indian tribe, *The Green-Eyed Indian*. She said she'd never read a novel with a positive view of Indian culture, so she wrote one. She has joined innumerable protests in the streets and at the southern border. Her advice to other activists: Always wear several pairs of underwear to a protest since you never know if you might be arrested.

Sally Alice has been a part of my life both as a friend and a social justice reformer with a sense of adventure, a tireless conscience, a playful sense of humor, and a huge heart. When I read that two women from the Center for Peace and Justice were writing a book about her and needed stories, I contacted them. For a year or so, Caroline Monie, Betsy Morrison, and I worked together, continuing interviews with fellow activists and friends. Then COVID-19 overtook an unprepared world and isolated us from one another. Friends set Sally Alice up with a bi-monthly Zoom connection, and she tuned in from her apartment at Brookdale, where she had recently moved. She was locked down for much of the pandemic. When life opened up again, Caroline and Betsy had both moved into new situations and could no longer continue the work. I was reluctant to work alone, and yet we'd already done so much—and I had never known Sally Alice to give up on a project. I decided to continue on my own.

Here is her story, contributed to by many who are awed by her vitality, resolve, and endurance. Despite the way the world seems to be moving in 2023, we believe her story needs to be shared to inspire and provide hope to those working to make the world a more just and compassionate place. Sally Alice shows us that looking beyond one's own problems, and working with and for others, can keep us vital and mentally sharp. As people live longer than ever, there is research today into why some people flourish and others languish as they age. Sally Alice is a living example of flourishing.

To create this book, we interviewed Sally Alice for hours, along with other influential people in her personal life and in the peace and justice community of Albuquerque. The task has been challenging because she has outlived her husband Don and their two children, her five younger siblings, and most of her peers. Today a "village" of people, nurtured through decades of working together, surrounds her to support and learn from her.

Who is Sally Alice Today?

Today, Sally Alice lives in Brookdale, a retirement community close to friends. But up until 2018 she lived in a large, two-story house that was unmistakably the home of someone who cared about our world. The grass had been replaced with synthetic lawn to save water, and the south side of the house provided solar energy through a tromb wall, maybe the first in town to use that early technology, she thinks. A "Bernie in 2016" sign hovered near the driveway, and another large sign posted on the turf displayed a quote from the Vatican: "Nuclear weapons are incompatible with the peace we seek for the 21st century." Out front there were often several cars parked as people assembled in the dining room with plans to change the world. Two steep steps led up to the front porch, but they didn't deter Sally Alice as she aged—she grasped the handholds at the bottom and swung herself up both steps several times a day. She mentioned her acupuncturist and the wonders he had worked with her knees each time she did it.

At the age of 99, she's a little stooped, but still tall and slim, elegant and dignified. Her smile is warm and welcoming, and her eyes behind the big heavy frames of her glasses still shine with an almost mischievous spirit. Her thick, unruly white hair tops a head full of ideas ready to escape and be shared. She loves to tease and be teased, or to provide a slightly off-color joke when she's invited. If the Raging Grannies are mentioned, she's ready to sing the most recent song she's written in a tremulous soprano.

In the early days of this project, Caroline Monie and I spent a lot of time sitting around Sally Alice's big kitchen table. Small bowls of chocolate and nuts offered a welcome to those gathered to talk about protests outside the gates of Kirtland Air Force Base, or which candidates to support in local elections. The coffee pot was always on, and Sally Alice was ready to engage.

The house had begun to crumble a bit by then, but it had once been the most imposing home on the block. She and her late husband Don bought it in the 1950s and added a second story. A huge bank of windows upstairs provided an expansive view of the Sandia Mountains to the east, glowing a warm watermelon pink with the rays of the setting sun. At night, those windows captured Albuquerque in its sparkling evening attire. It's a great room for a party with its spectacular view and plenty of seating, and she and Don hosted many. It also provided a haven for many fellow activists, trans women, and refugees needing a place to stay. Little had been done to the house since Don died in 2010, but at one time they swam in a pool in the backyard, now cracking in the sun, and Sally Alice raised chickens. Today the yard is overgrown, the apricot tree is dead, and weeds are coming up in the synthetic lawn.

The inside of the house reflected a woman too busy to spend a lot of time on something as mundane as housework. Fingerprints covered the kitchen cabinets, the sink was coffee-stained, and the smudges on the sliding doors to the patio blurred the green of the synthetic grass in the back yard. It was in this cozy, well-lived environment that Caroline and I began our chats with Sally Alice. Because she doesn't naturally call attention to herself, it took many interviews and increasingly specific questions to uncover the stories. She doesn't ramble or digress; she gets to the point quickly and concisely. Getting the details took probing. We were able to use some of the wall art from adopted grandchildren, awards she has received, and photos and souvenirs of her travels to inspire reminiscences. Coming from humble beginnings, she has remained humble her entire life.

Chapter 1

A dysfunctional family is any family with more than one person in it.

Mary Kerr, poet and essayist

Sally Alice was born Alice Thompson to Charles and Ellen Hollcroft on October 15, 1923, in rural Missouri. She added Sally to her name later when she felt Alice did not express who she truly is, and she will be Sally Alice throughout this memoir. She was the oldest of five children, four girls and, finally, a boy, in a Mennonite family. Her father was an itinerant day laborer during the Depression, moving the family often to find work, and they were dirt poor. Nutrition was as limited as conversation and expressions of affection.

The Mennonite faith dominated her childhood. Mennonites are Anabaptists, meaning believers are baptized as young people rather than infants. They are also pacifists who resist the violence of war. Her mother had grown up Mennonite, but her father was a convert, and, with the passion of a convert, he took his religion very seriously. He was jailed as a conscientious objector in World War I, and he continued to be a devout follower of his faith, reading only the Bible and Mennonite periodicals. All the children dressed in the traditional Mennonite way—for the girls, long dresses with long sleeves, sewn by their mother, and a hat on Sunday. These garments provoked bullying and torment on the playground. Sally Alice, like all Mennonite children, was baptized at about the age of 12, which meant she could take communion and participate in the foot-washing ritual, a symbol of the humility of Christ. As they washed one another's feet people were reminded to renounce worldly power and pride and offer their lives in humble service. Although the pacifist beliefs of her childhood remain with her today and she has served others with great humility all her life, Sally Alice says she was only "going through the motions" with the religion as a child and young adult. Later, she would renounce Christianity and work to create a Unitarian Universalist fellowship in Albuquerque based on humanist principles.

Her father believed that a second grade education was enough and that if you could read more than the Bible and could do more than multiply a few numbers, you were an "educated fool." He'd had smallpox as a child and never went back to school after second grade. He beat all the children frequently with a razor strap, even in bed, so they would cry themselves to sleep. As is so often the case, he was beaten by his own parents, who sent him out to cut the switches they beat him with. Sometimes, he confessed to Sally Alice as an adult, he made a small slice in the switch so it would break more quickly.

During the Depression, Charles struggled to support his growing family, and they had to move wherever he found work. He was fiercely self-sufficient and complained vociferously about unions and Franklin Roosevelt because they were "socialist." The children had little privacy and often all slept in the same bed. Sally Alice has no fond memories of any of the houses the family lived in. They never seemed to create a sense of a cozy home, but her mother did have a lead crystal sugar bowl and spoon holder that she treasured and everyone considered very special. With her sewing machine, Ellen made clothing for the children and herself from 25-pound flour sacks, even their underclothes when times were especially tough.

Despite her father's disdain for education, or maybe because of it, Sally Alice was a serious student and loved to read. Her weekly trips to the library and the stack of books near her bed opened the world to her. She dreamed of travel and of becoming a "heroine." Often late to school as she daydreamed along the way, she created worlds where she vanquished foes and fought for justice. Her father respected people who worked hard with their hands, but Sally Alice told him she was going to be a writer. She loved nothing more than a good story.

In the book she wrote years later, *Central Asia Fantasia,* she compares herself to the bumbling dreamer in "The Secret Life of Walter Mitty," a famous story by James Thurber about a man constantly distracted by his daydreams. She wrote, "I am Walter Mitty's real life female counterpart. I have always found my secret fantasies far preferable to the humdrum existence of 'real life,' where I felt myself relegated to the approximate value of a zero. I have never shared the wonderful details of my secret life, and in all probability, no one will ever know about my many satisfying experiences in which I am the undeniable, unqualified heroine."

Those dreams led her to defy or ignore her family's values every chance she got. At one point her father worked for the railroad and her family lived in a compound with the Anglo boss and a Mexican family. Her parents forbid her from playing with those "Papists" next door who attended a Catholic church. They followed orders from that Pope in Rome and ate blood pudding! Sally Alice paid no attention and played with the children anyway. She liked them more than the boss's son, who was a big bully, and she wondered how different ways of worshipping God could cut people off from one another.

Sally Alice always felt different from all the other children around her—the kids at school who teased her relentlessly and those in her own family. She was closest to her sister Glada, who was younger by two years. They walked to school together and dressed in one another's clothes as teens, yet there was plenty of sibling rivalry. Glada was considered the "pretty one," so Sally Alice claimed she was smarter and a better singer. One time Sally Alice broke a window while playing with neighbor kids. When her father came home, she told him Glada had done it, so he ran upstairs and whipped Glada with his razor strap. She cried and told him Sally Alice had lied, so Sally Alice also got the strap. But she didn't mind the whipping nearly as much because Glada had gotten it, too. So there!

Very few of Sally Alice's memories of childhood are of warmth and love. She remembers her father holding other children but never his own. It felt to her like his own were never good enough for him, and the whippings with his razor strap did little to contradict this feeling. One time she overheard a conversation with children from another family who were talking about which child in the family loved their mother the most. Sally Alice was amazed—until that moment, she had never thought of parents as sources or recipients of love! "Antagonism" was the word she used to describe her relationship with her parents. She realized that they were gentler with the children if they were sick, so she coughed a lot as a child, but with five of them, attention was still in short supply.

However, there was a time when Sally Alice remembers her father showing what might be interpreted as compassion for his children. As the younger children began school, each of them came home with stories of bullying on the playground for being different and dressing strangely. All of them were called "Hog Trough", mimicking the pronunciation of Hollcroft, their last name. Finally, perhaps in exasperation with all the whining, perhaps in sympathy, Sally Alice's father changed the pronunciation of their name to "Wholecroft," with a long "o." Miraculously, this simple switch alleviated at least some of the bullying.

Sally Alice says she lived "at the end of the time of women being property." Her mother was subservient to her father and didn't question his child-rearing practices. She, too, was emotionally remote. When Sally Alice was about 8, she invited her mother to a tea party. She'd read about a tea party in *Alice in Wonderland,* so she carefully prepared the table with teacups, the lead crystal sugar bowl, a pot of hot water and a few wildflowers in the middle of the table. Eagerly, she sat down to pour the tea and chat with her mother. Suddenly, her mother stood up and said, "I think I'd better start getting dinner ready." Sally Alice sat mute with disappointment. Other attempts at conversation were usually met with a simple, "Hush." (Originally, I wrote "hush, dear" here, but when Sally Alice read it, she told me her mother would have never used a word like "dear.") She never had a birthday cake until she was 16, and it was made by a woman she stayed with when her parents made another move and she hadn't wanted to change schools again.

In addition to the five siblings, one baby had been stillborn and one had died in infancy before Sally Alice came along. These children, Opal and Leta, were "angels" to her parents and referred to by name often in their perfection. Sally Alice was jealous because she wanted to be an "angel," but her parents always found something to criticize. As a teen wanting to fit in and to be pretty like her sister, she once bought some nail polish and painted her nails. When her father saw it, he handed her a paring knife and demanded that she remove every last bit with the knife. Sitting at the dinner table, he watched intently as she slowly and painfully scraped it off, holding back the tears.

The children were curious about sex, especially when a new baby arrived in the family every couple of years. When they were sent to sleep at Grandma's, there could be a new sibling when they came back. Their mother told the girls about menstruation, but could not bring herself to go any further. Even the word "bull," with its connotations of testosterone and virility, embarrassed her, so all male cattle were called "steers." Corn silk reminded her of pubic hair, so she hated to husk corn. Sally Alice was left to try to figure out the truth about sex through playground rumors and gossip, so when she left home at 19, she was extremely naïve about it.

Tasks like cooking for the family and looking after the younger children often fell to Sally Alice. She had to wash diapers by bringing in the firewood, heating water on the wood stove, soaking them, and then washing them on a washboard and hanging them out to dry. Because her mother was so often pregnant or nursing, she was also the main bread baker—a simple white bread made with flour, yeast, and lard. The yeast was kept going by adding a little sugar. Meals usually consisted of one main dish, often just cornbread and milk or navy beans and milk. Her father's opinions dominated even the kitchen, and because he didn't like onions or garlic, no dishes were ever made with them. Today Sally Alice is known for being able to throw together a tasty, nutritious meal, including plenty of onions and garlic, while talking on the phone or chatting with a visitor.

As she grew older, Sally Alice's isolation from those around her continued. Her family "ganged up" on her, in her own words, because even then she wasn't comfortable with their religious beliefs and practices. She came to believe it was her fault for being different, contributing to her low self-esteem as she headed into her teen years. She wasn't allowed to attend social activities like the prom, and she missed a lot of school her senior year because of appendicitis.

Recently I discovered Mariam Toews, a Canadian writer who grew up Mennonite in a small town in Alberta, Canada. In her book, *A Complicated Kindness*, she created a character whose life reflects what she must have experienced in the family and community she grew up in. Toews writes about the founder of the Mennonite religion, Menno:

> We're Mennonites. As far as I know, we are the most embarrassing sub-sect of people to belong to if you're a teenager. . . Imagine the least well-adjusted kid in your school starting a breakaway clique of people whose manifesto includes a ban on media, dancing, smoking, temperate climates, movies, drinking, rock n roll, having sex for fun, swimming, make-up, jewelry, playing pool, going to cities, or staying up past 9 o'clock. That was Menno all over.

From *A Complicated Kindness* by Miriam Toews

In spite of such beliefs, that feisty streak of Sally Alice's showed itself early on when she heard about a program funded by the New Deal, Franklin Roosevelt's set of government programs for tackling the Depression. The National Youth Administration focused on helping young people stay in school by providing them with a way to make money. Sally Alice pestered her school principal about this until he finally agreed to allow his students to join. Then she and sister Glada graded papers and sold candy bars, earning $3 a month to help them buy school clothes and supplies. She also worked in a tomato cannery to earn money in high school, giving her paycheck to her father each week.

Sally Alice generally spoke critically of her father, labeling her childhood as traumatic when asked to talk about her early years, but once I asked her if, looking back, she could feel some compassion for his lot in life. She stared out the window for few moments before telling me of how the family at one time had moved from Kansas to Versailles, Missouri, and were met at the train station by her father in a horse and buggy. He took them to live in a two-story house with only the kitchen stove for heat and boards missing from the upstairs. Those boards never got fixed because he was too busy and tired from keeping the small farm going. They had a vegetable garden, chickens, three cows, and a cream separator, and they lived on what they got from selling the cream. The farm was inadequately financed and all the implements, including the tractor, were old and broken. Charles worked hard, but when the cows died from eating lead paint in the garage, there was no recovering. When he lost the farm, Sally Alice left home. She had loved those cows, she said. Maybe she also loved her father and used this story to say that she was filled with too much sorrow for him to remain at home. She couldn't really explain. She was just 19.

Chapter 2

There comes a time in your life when you have to choose to turn the page, write another book, or simply close it.

Sharon L. Alder, therapist and writer

In those days on the prairie, it was possible to get a teaching certificate by completing certain courses in high school, which allowed young people to become eligible to teach after graduating and turning 18. Sally Alice, crazy for independence and autonomy, gratefully completed the preparation and graduated with a teaching credential good for two years. After graduation, she helped a more experienced teacher until her 18th birthday. Then she took on her first solo assignment, eagerly replacing a teacher whose lesson plans had focused on recess most of the day. Those eighth grade students felt ill-prepared and fearful they wouldn't pass the exams to graduate. But Sally Alice stepped in toward the end of the school year, and within weeks had organized the classroom and motivated students so that all of them were able to graduate on time.

Her first assignment as a full-fledged teacher was in a one-room schoolhouse where she had eight students, ranging from first grade through eighth grade. She was a conscientious teacher. She had textbooks, though no access to a library, but her love of books served her well. Her goal was to get her students to think for themselves. A teacher-training instructor, recognizing great potential in her, said she would pay Sally Alice's way to college at the end of the school year. But she was only 19 and living a lonely existence in a rented apartment. Innocently, she allowed a precocious eighth grade girl and some boys, just a few years younger than she was, to become friends. When word got out that she was hanging out with students, the offer of college was withdrawn. Teachers have always been expected to create a respectful distance between themselves and their students so as not to be accused of playing favorites, but Sally Alice's youth and isolation won out over more professional behavior. With the withdrawal of support from her supervising teacher, hope of being a college student disappeared.

At the end of the school year she was required to renew her teaching credential, but that meant taking some college classes that she couldn't afford. Unwilling to return home, she struck out on her own and moved to Davenport, an Iowa town on the Mississippi River. Davenport had been hit hard by the Depression but was on its way to better days, thanks to the economic boom created by World War II and the Works Project Administration (WPA), another of Roosevelt's New Deal programs. Sally Alice took any job that came along—waiting tables, factory work in a foundry where she was the only woman—and lived in rented rooms. Since her Mennonite faith had ingrained in her that almost anything pleasurable was a sin and the biggest sin was renouncing God, she thought to herself, "I'm never going to get into heaven so I might as well sin big!" Thus began the period in her life that she is least proud of—a period of loneliness and lack of direction caused by no sense of self-esteem and little to believe in, most importantly herself. She filled the void with relationships with men, allowing them to use her physically and emotionally. She hung out in bars, where men picked her up and took her home. Because she hadn't learned about sex from her parents, she filled in the blanks with each new experience with a man. Commitment was never a part of these relationships—just the temporary fix of overcoming loneliness for a few days or weeks. Looking back, she says it was the most terrifying time of her life.

She knew she was lost but she didn't feel like she had any choices. Finally with World War II raging around her, Sally Alice realized that she could rebel even further against her pious, conscientious-objector father—she could join the military and make a living doing it! In 1944 she joined the Navy and made it through boot camp at Hunter College. Boot camp for women in those days was nothing like the strenuous physical requirements of today. She remembers it as "neatness training," where the main goal was to keep your underwear drawer organized and tidy. She also remembers marching in formation and standing for inspection for hours, but she never handled a gun. After boot camp she was sent to Samson, New York, to learn how to handle military mail.

Women were needed for the war effort and for the first time she felt she was doing something important. She was helping fight fascism, she thought, and protecting the country that was protecting the world. She was doing her small part for democracy. It felt good. She had swallowed "the poison," as she put it, but it didn't last long. Within a couple months, Sally Alice discovered she was pregnant, and when the Navy found out, she was forced to leave with an honorable discharge. Not knowing who the father was, she gave the baby up for adoption, never even knowing its gender. She states this very matter-of-factly with little emotion after more than 70 years of living with this fact.

Once again, she didn't know which way to turn. The Navy had given her a brief sense of purpose and meaning, and then it all came to an abrupt and traumatic end. She didn't have to wonder about her future for long, though. With the end of the war in 1945 came an incredible opportunity called the G.I. Bill.

The G.I. Bill, or the Serviceman's Readjustment Act of 1944, made available low- cost mortgages, low-interest business and farm loans, and payment of tuition and living expenses for high school, college, or vocational school to veterans who had served at least 90 days. (Shockingly, Black veterans did not receive home or business loans). While President Roosevelt had wanted to put qualifying requirements on the benefits, the American Legion lobbied for benefits to be available more broadly. Having thought that her chance for college was long gone, Sally Alice qualified for education benefits based on her six months of service in the Navy. She jumped at this opportunity and immediately enrolled at University of Iowa in Davenport to major in general science and education.

Her sister Lois lived in Chicago. Lois was less religious and more fun than her other siblings, and she and Sally Alice stayed in touch, visiting one another now and then. While she was a student, Sally Alice made a life-changing trip to visit Lois, who had a boyfriend named Bob. He'd

been wounded in the Navy and sent to a hospital in Alexandria, Egypt. There he met Don Thompson, another Navy vet injured in the war. Their similar fates and their Chicago roots drew them close, and they left the hospital good friends before heading back home. Don enrolled at University of Illinois under the G.I. Bill, and Bob met Lois, who became his wife.

One summer day, tall, slim, athletic Don was at his job as lifeguard at a Lake Michigan beach. Suddenly the sound of a motorcycle broke through the lull of the surf and children's laughter. Looking down from his tall chair, he saw Bob with a woman on the back of his motorbike. Bob

Young Don

called up to him, "What are you doing tonight? Want to double date with Lois here and her sister Alice? She's in town from University of Iowa." Don inspected Lois and agreed.

That night the two couples had dinner downtown in the Loop and walked along the shore of the lake. Don and Sally Alice chattered non-stop to one another, almost oblivious of Bob and Lois. Finally, Bob and Lois were ready to call it a night, but Don and Sally Alice weren't. As she remembers it, they talked the rest of the night, excited about being in college and the lives that awaited them after the war—and also excited about each other.

Sally Alice had never met a man so articulate and thoughtful and interested in who she was and what she thought. They talked of Don's horrific experiences of being shelled by the Germans off the coast of Salerno, Italy, from the landing ship he was stationed on. His shipmates were killed, and he was filled with shrapnel. After experiencing such horror, Don told her, "There can't be a God." These conversations were the first of many that began to peel the veil from Sally Alice's eyes about war and US involvement in the world. She'd known nothing of the Japanese internment camps, and she had celebrated along with other Americans when the bomb was dropped on Hiroshima. Later she came to believe the bomb had not been necessary to win the war.

The two continued to see one another as they each pursued their dream of a college degree. Sally Alice was excited about her classes and did very well in the ones she loved like embryology; nev-

Don and Sally Alice cut their wedding cake

ertheless, she was still young, the war was over, and people were eager to cast aside the hardship and heartache it had brought. She graduated with a degree in education and science but says, "I wish I'd studied more and partied less." She'd dreamed of medical school, but her 2.5 grade point average wasn't good enough to get in.

Don graduated with a degree in Spanish. By this time, he had left the

Navy but continued with the Naval Reserves in order to be eligible for a pension later. He left with the rank of Ensign Lieutenant JG and returned to the Reserves once a month for training until he retired. While he was in training with the Reserves one summer, Sally Alice got a job at a mental institution in New York. She still remembers after more than 70 years how he came to visit one weekend, and when she tried to introduce him to her colleagues, she couldn't remember his name. She laughs heartily when she tells this story. They met when they could and continued what Sally Alice described as a friendship, even though Don often would say, "When we get married we can do 'this or that.'" I asked her if there was a physical side of their relationship because the word friendship was always used when she talked about Don, and she answered rather indignantly, "Well, of course there was!" But still, Sally Alice considered Don's marriage comments to be jokes between good friends until one night when he said, "You *are* going to marry me, aren't you?" Her stomach dropped and her heart thumped but it didn't take her long to decide. The more romantic side to pragmatic Sally Alice appeared when she told me they'd wanted to marry on Valentine's Day in 1950, but the church couldn't accommodate them. They were married a week later in a Unitarian Universalist church in the company of parents, siblings, and a few friends.

Chapter 3

I'm selfish, impatient and a little insecure. I make mistakes, I am out of control and at times hard to handle. But if you can't handle me at my worst, then you sure as hell don't deserve me at my best.

Marilyn Monroe, actor

Sally Alice says, "Don changed my life by making me feel wanted." After their wedding, they returned to Urbana, Illinois, while he worked on a master's in Spanish at University of Illinois. Like her, Don had been poor as a child. During the Depression, his father worked as an electrician and the family moved around into apartments with move-in specials for a month of free or reduced rent. Don played baseball and swam in Lake Michigan with his one brother, who later moved to Albuquerque. He was a competitive swimmer in high school. Although he sometimes displayed a temper, Don was most often described by friends of the couple as good-hearted, smart, handsome, and charismatic. He loved to laugh and tease. He could give a speech in Spanish, play the guitar, and swim for miles.

Sally Alice came up with one word to illustrate their marriage: complex. "Complex because of personal idiosyncrasies and shared stupidity. What helped it survive were mutual admiration and respect," she added. The story of their long marriage of 61 years shows a shared streak of independence from the very start. Not long after they were married,

Don left for Mexico City to study Spanish literature as part of his graduate work, leaving his bride alone. I asked her what the discussion was like
around Don's desire to study in Mexico, and she said there was none. "He
just told me he was going," she said. While some of Sally Alice's women
friends were aghast, she took it in stride, and it seems to have set the tone
for the whole marriage. She tells the story of a time when a protest of some
kind was being planned and a woman asked her if her husband would let
her go. "I've never asked him. I just go," she replied in surprise.

Housing after the war was hard to come by, so at first they lived with
an elderly woman and helped look after her house. She had a coal furnace
that worried her daily, and Don would tease her relentlessly about strange
noises or smells coming from the basement. Finally, they left and moved
into student housing,then bought a very small trailer with no bathroom
and lived in a trailer park.

They didn't have much time to relax and enjoy life before the shadow of
the Korean War fell over them and Don was called back to the west coast
to train with the Reserves. They set out from Urbana with their trailer
pulled by the "junker" car they'd bought, but quickly realized that the car
wasn't strong enough to pull the trailer, nor did they have insurance or
titles for either one. "We were so naïve!" laughed Sally Alice. They returned
to Urbana, found the titles, and traded the car in for a pickup truck. Not
long after setting out the second time, the trailer was hit by a truck and
totaled. Sally Alice's parents arrived on the scene to help them reorganize
their belongings, and at last they arrived in San Francisco, having left many
possessions behind.

Determined to have fun despite the second war in their short relationship, they rented a bare-bones apartment where they shared a single bed,
using the money they saved to travel up and down the coast and go to plays
and concerts. "We had a ball," said Sally Alice. "This was most carefree
time of our marriage." Sometimes they hung out with officers, and one
evening, the commanding officer wanted to come to their apartment to
hear Don play the guitar. They tried desperately to distract him from visiting their cheap, tiny home, but he came anyway. He left impressed by their

simple, thrifty lifestyle, and especially impressed at how they cuddled up in a single bed.

The Korean War is often called the Forgotten War, even though 40,000 US troops died, many more were injured, and close to 5 million Korean civilians were killed. Perhaps it has been almost forgotten because it accomplished very little, although it did ensure that South Korea did not become communist. Many of the mistakes in this war were repeated later in Vietnam and Afghanistan. During negotiations after WWII, Korea had been divided randomly at the 38th parallel, the USSR being given the north and the US the south. Since the US had no military or commercial interests there at the time, Korea was pretty much ignored until Kim Il Sung, the communist ruler in the north installed by the Soviets, massed troops with the support of the Soviets to invade the south in an attempt at unification. The Cold War against communism was in full swing, and the US quickly reacted to this communist threat by sending troops to join the UN peacekeeping force there. In fact, that force was made up largely of American troops. When North Korea began pushing south toward Seoul, those troops became embroiled in fighting from June 1950 through July 1953, at one time taking on Chinese troops that had come to help North Korea. In the end, Korea remained divided at the 38th parallel.

As a member of the Navy reserves, Don was sent to Hawaii, where he boarded the USS Taylor, a destroyer escort sent to the west coast of Korea. He left a pregnant Sally Alice in Honolulu. She got a job in the neo-natal unit of a hospital and joined a supportive group of military wives also left behind. They were wonderfully helpful throughout her pregnancy and after the birth of Sarita in 1952. Don didn't return to Honolulu until the war was over in July 1953, when Sarita was several months old. Sally Alice laughs when she tells of the time after his return when Don wanted to go to a party, and she pointed out that they didn't have a babysitter. "That's ok," Don replied. "We can just put her in the trunk." Together they learned about parenting their new baby, although Sally Alice nursed her and did most of the hands-on care, like most women did in the 1950s.

Don returned horrified by war once again. The USS Taylor was a destroyer escort that patrolled the coast of Korea, shelling North Korean artillery batteries and lines of transport. Innocent civilians lived in and among these targets, and he hated being complicit in the killing and destruction. At times, Chinese tailors attempted to board the ship, looking for opportunities to make clothing for the troops, but all Chinese had been deemed the communist enemy. The tailors were swept off the ship into the frigid waters of the sea with blasts from water hoses. Don carried these images in his mind for the rest of his life, hating the fact that war had to create "the other," the enemy, as less than human.

But he and his young wife had a new baby, and they needed a nest. Deciding to return to the familiar Midwest, they headed for Urbana, Illinois, with a nest egg of $6,800 from the settlement on the totaled trailer and savings from Don's paycheck to help them get started. Passing through Albuquerque, they bought a paper in the morning over breakfast at the top of Nine Mile Hill. Incredibly, there was a classified ad for a fully furnished house on Utah Street NE for sale for exactly $6,800! It felt like a sign from the universe. Heading down Route 66 with the sun rising over the Sandia Mountains and the city spread before them, they agreed this would be a fine place to live for a while. They bought that house.

Chapter 4

*Call it a clan, call it a network, call it a tribe, call it a family: What-
ever you call it, whoever you are, you need one.*

Jane Howard, journalist and biographer

A s they settled into their new home and life, the young couple began
to explore ideas that would help propel their country and community into more peaceful and equitable times. Don became a high school
Spanish teacher, and, for a short time, Sally Alice served on the police
force in Albuquerque. She was one of two women hired that year, and although she did target practice during training, she refused to carry a gun
on duty. The police were not "gun happy" in those days, she said—their
biggest fear was organized crime. After two years of earnest efforts, Sally
Alice decided this was not the career for her—she still had a lot of faith
in people and didn't like regarding everyone with suspicion. She quit
and decided to take the necessary classes to get a New Mexico teaching
certificate.

One of the only people still alive who has known Sally Alice since
she was a young woman is Mandy Pino, another 97-year-old wonder.
Pino lives in a retirement community but remains active with Progressive Democrats of America, focusing on reforming health care. She met
Sally Alice and Don in the 1950s, through work with a grassroots committee of the Democrat party that started with eight people and even-

tually grew to 25 members. The group was considered radical by other Democrats. They met regularly and hashed out burning issues till three in the morning. The fossil fuel and liquor industries ran New Mexico at the time, and the powerful Democratic Party controlled liquor sales, granting expensive licenses to a few select people. The party was a political machine run by "bosses" who stayed in power through bought votes. Their grassroots committee opposed this patronage system and worked hard to end it. The group interviewed every candidate who was running and then canvassed door to door, handing out little packets of grass seed (grass roots organizing) to promote the ones they agreed with. During political rallies they had a megaphone and shouted, "Take the money and vote as you please!" By the early 1960s, the group had helped to elect eight out of nine county commissioners, and things began to change. According to Mandy, Don was politically ambitious from the start (he would later run for the state senate); Sally Alice was quiet and laid back but always independent and true to herself, working largely behind the scenes to make sure things got done. And they always did. People could count on her.

Although Don and Sally Alice shared many similar values and allowed one another to be independent, both had entered the marriage with baggage from their early years and recognized they could use some help. They joined a co-counseling group that helped people become peer counselors, guiding one another through difficult times by emphasizing that feelings are not who we are—we can move beyond them. They made lasting friends through this group of people who had been able to become so vulnerable with one another.

While busy with their jobs and local organizing, their family expanded with the birth of Del. Sarita's name was a Spanish diminutive of Sarah, the name of FDR's mother, and Del was short for Delano, FDR's middle name. Don continued to teach Spanish, and Sally Alice stayed home with the two children. She has admitted that she never really planned to have children, but once Sarita was born, they thought she should have a sibling. It took her nine years to get pregnant again.

Mandy remembers how the two families brought their children to organizing events to play together while the adults worked. When Sarita turned 10, she was often left to babysit for Del.

Several friends from that period said that Don and Sally Alice didn't seem to know a lot about raising children. Considering their hard-scrabble childhoods during the Depression, this maybe isn't surprising. As Sally Alice claims, she and her siblings raised each other and spent a large part of their childhoods climbing trees and roaming the neighborhood. Nevertheless, she and Don loved their children and did their best to provide them with security and broadening experiences. Every summer they took camping trips around the country to national parks and regions with cultural variations like the deep South. Sally Alice, a real dog lover, likes to tell the story of Chico, their small dog who joined them on one of these trips to visit friends in New Orleans. When they

The professional Sally Alice

went to dinner one night, they left him in the car, but somehow he got out and disappeared. Heartbroken, they searched the area for hours to no avail, but when they got home, there he was at the front door. He'd found his way back to them in a completely unfamiliar city!

Sarita seemed to be a happy child when she was young, playing often with neighborhood children. She was very fond of her father and called him Daddy. Don enjoyed taking her on errands with him, and every year they went to the hardware store to look at the Christmas decorations and

21

toys. Sarita was also close to her mother, especially the one year that she and Sally Alice were home alone during the week, when Don taught fourth grade 40 miles south of Albuquerque, and only came home on weekends. But when asked about which parent her daughter most resembled, Sally Alice replied, "She was very much an individual, not like either of us."

By the time she reached adolescence Sarita's individuality had turned into rebelliousness. She wanted to grow up fast—drinking cough syrup, dressing maturely, being lazy in school in spite of being bright. She ran away several times, had a baby at 15, and gave him up for adoption. The first time she ran away, she tried to cross the border into Mexico, but an immigration agent notified Sally Alice and Don. She tried again and this time made it to Haight Ashbury, a neighborhood of San Francisco. In the mid-1960s, Haight Ashbury was notorious for young people coming of age in an atmosphere of "free love," music, marijuana, and psychedelic drugs. Sally Alice tried to find her daughter several times. One evening there was a dead cat on the front porch of their house, and Sally Alice suddenly had a vision of Sarita, lying dead somewhere. She sobbed for hours.

When Sarita finally returned home, she was addicted to drugs. Sally Alice believes that the drugs changed her whole nervous system. She struggled with and was treated for mental health issues, becoming paranoid and hearing voices for the rest of her life. Sally Alice and Don helped get her into rehab, and paid for her to take college classes, but nothing helped for long. She was a beautiful young woman and a talented artist, but she never managed to get her life back on track.

Shortly before Sally Alice's move to a retirement community, we sat down together to look through some photograph albums she had unearthed as she prepared for the estate sale. The first one we picked up from the pile was titled DEL. My heart thumped and I imagined hers did, too. I knew Del had taken his own life at a young age, but we hadn't yet talked about that painful topic. We opened the book and began looking at photos of a chubby, smiling little boy. The photos inspired stories. He was such a joy as a child, Sally Alice said—even-tempered and adventurous and he had a great love of animals of all kinds. He was always bringing some living creature home with him: spiders in boxes, bright-eyed lizards, injured birds he wanted to save. One time he found a puppy about eight weeks old, and they played ball and ran around in the backyard all afternoon. That night he took it to bed with him, and in the morning, she heard his wail of grief from upstairs. He had rolled over and suffocated the puppy during the night. It took them both days to get over that heartbreak.

He played Little League baseball and she and Don took him to many Albuquerque Dukes baseball games over the years. He always wanted to catch a baseball at Lobo Stadium, but never did—and he never caught a fish either, in spite of all the times they spent at Fenton Lake in the forests of the Jemez Mountains. Like any mother, Sally Alice hated to see him disappointed.

Del seemed to get along with everyone. When he was about 10, Sally Alice's sister-in-law died, and she and Don took in their five small boys for about six weeks. They were squeezed onto every mattress and couch in their house. Del pitched in to become an older brother, and the boys loved him. They rode bikes, hunted butterflies, picked apricots, and ate like whales. Del made the whole situation much easier until the children went to live with an aunt. They never had to go to foster care.

Del was passionate about technology and read a lot of science fiction. Once he built a hot air balloon that actually rose up in the air. He breathlessly watched as it climbed about 10 feet, then caught fire and floated to the ground. He was thrilled. When he was 12, he won third prize in a Lego contest by building a missile launcher. Even though she and Don constantly talked to him about the death and destruction caused by war and weapons and never allowed him to have a gun, he was fascinated with the military.

Some of the best time Sally Alice spent with him was traveling through Europe when Del was about 10. She bought a Karmann Ghia (if you can believe Sally Alice in a sporty little car like that!) in Portugal, and the two of them drove across Spain, Italy, Austria, Germany, France, and the Netherlands. He was a great traveler and sat for hours in the car, eyes shining as they passed windmills and castles and riverboats. Once though, Sally Alice left him at a guest house while she went to find something to eat and she got lost. She was terrified that she'd never get back to him, but after some panicked searching, she found the place. They "roamed through Rome, had pizza in Pisa, and went insane on the Seine." They even stayed in a castle for two nights. *Europe on $5 a Day* was their trusted resource.

Don and Sally Alice took Del back to Europe again three years later and stayed in Servas homes. Servas was an organization whose members hosted one another when they were traveling in the US and internationally. They hosted a lot of people at their home in Albuquerque and always had interesting experiences as hosts and guests. They returned to Europe together a third time to chaperone a group of students. However, they realized Del was beginning to think that Europe was the center of the universe, so their next trip was to the northeast US, where he could get to know some of America and its history.

Despite all his parents' anti-war activism and advice, Del joined the Air Force after he got a GED. They tried to talk him out of it and proposed he join the Coast Guard instead, but Sally Alice said, "I suppose it was a way to rebel against his parents, as young people so often have to do. After all, I joined the Navy at Del's age, partly for three meals a day and a paycheck but partly to spite my father, the conscientious objector." Del went off to boot camp and ended up stationed in North Dakota, working with information technology. They didn't hear a lot from him, and they were busy with their lives.

Many interviews later, I found out that Sally Alice had learned of Del's death while on a peace march through the Soviet Union. The news that he had taken his own life made it even more painful. "I can't even begin to describe the shock of losing a child like that." Sally Alice said. "After I heard that, I kind of lost it." She was unable to complete the 30-hour journey back to the US in time for his funeral in Albuquerque and his burial in the Santa Fe Veterans Cemetery.

She and Don stayed close after this tragedy. They blamed themselves and yet knew that Del had set his own course when he joined the military.

"Memories of the good times come flooding back as you wonder what went wrong. I asked myself what I could have done differently. I wished we'd been in closer touch so I would have known that he was struggling with something," she said. They never thought he was cut out for military life, but they could only speculate as to what pushed him to that final step. "He was a child of the desert with days of light and sunshine being a part of his growing up," she mused. He'd requested a transfer many times from the damp cold and grey of North Dakota and never gotten it. She also wonders if he might have been gay in a very intolerant military at the time. Sally Alice still ponders the reasons, but through the years, she's learned to keep breathing and put one foot in front of the other. In her eyes, time heals and the grief becomes less stabbing, but it never fully retreats. A few weeks after his death, they received a program from the memorial service the military provided, and he was given a meritorious service medal.

Here is a poem Sally Alice wrote after his death. She's not a religious person, she pointed out, but she has found throughout her life that writing really helps to explore feelings and bring some solace.

To Del

Fly, fly gentle spirit, fly!
And let your heavy anguish
Fall away behind.
Soar. beloved one, soar!
And be at peace
Completely unconfined.
But let our love
Rest lightly on your wings
To keep you warm
On long cold nights.
Remember us if you can
And have a joyous flight.

As an adult, Sarita continued to struggle with mental health issues, living on Social Security Supplemental Income. For the last ten years of her life, she lived with a man named Johnnie in Albuquerque. She was quite paranoid and convinced that Johnnie would kill her or throw her out eventually, so she saved $6,000 and put it in a safe deposit box which was found after her death. Her relationship with her parents was tenuous. Although they paid for college, therapy, and drug rehabilitation when it was needed, they

were not close. In 30 years of friendship with Don and Sally Alice, I never met Sarita, and only heard vague mention of a daughter somewhere. A friend who lived with Sally Alice and Don for a time would have liked a friendship with her, but Sarita didn't reach

Sally Alice and Don with Sarita

back. She was anti-social and didn't like her parents' friends. She resented the fact that her parents had built a swimming pool after she'd moved out of the house so Don could keep up his swimming ability for the Senior Olympics. She blew in and out of their lives when it suited her.

Sadly, Sarita died at the age of 66 from health issues brought on by her lifestyle. When it was decided that she would be taken off life support in the hospital, Sally Alice moaned, "Oh, my beautiful baby!" Don had also passed on by this time, and she was distraught. When I asked what she needed, what I could do to help, she answered, "Can you make the time go faster?" A close friend observed that she seemed to grieve for Sarita even more than Don. Sarita's obituary shows a photo of a very attractive woman but provides no description of her life. Three of only six pieces of framed art Sally Alice took to the retirement community were painted by Sarita.

Never Turning Back

Although Sally Alice still questions where she went wrong as a parent of her own children, family can come in many forms. Teachers rarely know what lasting influence they've had on their students, but Gwenyth, one of her fourth grade students, became like a daughter and is still in touch with her after more than 60 years.

Gwenyth bustled into my house on a breath of cold air, full of energy and eager to share stories about Sally Alice. Her enthusiasm and her tales of her many experiences in other countries as observer and activist showed me right away why they had remained friends for so many years. Quiet and scared as a child, Gwenyth had grown up similar to Sally Alice—few friends and a lonely, isolated life as a latch key kid with a father who sometimes beat her. During an exercise with multiplication tables one day, Gwenyth wrote over and over on the back of her paper, "I wish I was dead." Sally Alice must have sensed her unhappiness because she turned the paper over to read the back, and immediately intervened to find Gwenyth some support at school. Another teacher also volunteered to take Gwenyth home when she needed to get away for a while.

Once Gwenyth knew Sally Alice had her back, she was able to relax and learn in a classroom filled with posters of Machu Picchu and other far away places, and tons of books. The kids put on a memorable show called The Planets in which students played the roles of planets in the solar system, dancing around the sun to music, and some, including Gwenyth, were chosen to learn to play the autoharp. She remembers vividly the many books, bright classroom, and story times, as well as that Sally Alice never required her students to say the Pledge of Allegiance. They were encouraged to think for themselves and question everything. These experiences helped to shape Gwenyth's choices as an adult, and she and Sally Alice grew to have even more in common.

Gwenyth married and moved away for a number of years and then returned to Albuquerque. She knew to look for Sally Alice through the Center for Peace and Justice, and the two were delighted to be together again. Sally Alice had begun attending the School of the Americas Watch, a group of US citizens who traveled each year to the School of the Americas (a.k.a. School of Assassins) at Fort Benning, GA, now called the Western Hemisphere Institute for Security Cooperation. The goal of this group was to inform people in the US of the deadly role the US was playing in training Central American military and security personnel. According to the group, these personnel were often recruited by the US to subvert legally-elected governments the US considered unfriendly to US economic interests. Sally Alice was one of seven who had shown up for the first protest in Georgia, but the movement gathered support over the years. Terrorism perpetrated in Honduras, El Salvador, and other Central American countries by personnel trained at SOA has been part of the cause of mass migrations to our borders from these countries; thus, the protests have been moved to our border with Mexico in recent times.

One year Gwenyth drove down through New Mexico to the protest with Sally Alice. An explosive sound startled them and at first, they thought there was a helicopter overhead. Finally, they realized there was a problem with the car, so they pulled over and waited three hours, laughing and talking nonstop, until help arrived. When the blowout was repaired, they continued down to the border, where everyone ran to greet Sally Alice. Gwenyth said these occasions were multi-generational and fun, even as they protested the grim reality of US intervention in Central America.

Sally Alice's family grew in another way one day when her phone rang as she was cooking dinner for her friend Mandy. A surprised "Wow!" from Sally Alice as she listened to the voice on the other end alerted Mandy that something unusual was up. The conversation that followed revealed that Sarita's son, Eric, given up for adoption by Sarita years before, was in search of his birth family, and he'd found Sally Alice through a second cousin in a "23 and Me" search. The cousin helped him find Sarita's family in Albuquerque, as well as his birth father. After Eric and his wife Alexis googled Sally Alice, they wanted to meet her. So Eric made the call. Sarita wanted nothing to do with him, but his birth father did, and so did Sally Alice. She delightedly became a grandma overnight.

Eric was adopted at birth on July 29, 1967. As his birth father told him later, he was a product of "the summer of love" when Sarita was just 15. He had a happy childhood with loving parents and an adopted brother 14 months younger. Like all adopted children, he wondered about his birth parents, and "23 and Me" provided the opportunity to investigate. He didn't tell his adoptive parents, not wanting to seem ungrateful, but he figured his adoptive father suspected. He found that his birth father sold art online in California. Saying he was interested in buying a painting, Eric contacted him, and gradually, as they negotiated the deal, the truth came out. His father was open to a meeting, and the relationship grew from there. Eric said his father loved music, was creative and produced shows at a TV station. They met quite often before his father's death, and Eric bought several art pieces from him.

Eric is married to Alexis, a finance attorney, and they live in New York City with their daughter, Savana. Eric's phone call has led to a close relationship. Eric and Alexis have come to Albuquerque, and they have arranged to meet Sally Alice in Utah, where each of them has friends or family. Sally Alice has artwork for "Grandma" from her new great-grandchild hanging on her walls. Many Saturdays beginning with the COVID epidemic, Alexis has helped set up and participates in a Zoom call for Sally Alice's friends and family. Alexis says Sally Alice inspires her to be a better person because of her strong values and activism.

Through the years, Sally Alice has worked with Bob Anderson, a Vietnam War veteran and instructor at Albuquerque's local community college, and his wife, Jeanne Pahls, a dynamic and progressive teacher in Albuquerque. Bob started an organization called Stop the War Machine, whose members demonstrated against war and nuclear weapons outside the gates of Kirtland Air Force Base for many years. Bob also ran for Congress with the Green Party but lost. When Don and Sally Alice founded the local chapter of Veterans for Peace, Bob joined their efforts, and since Don died, they have gathered most Sundays for dinner and shared important celebrations. Bob and Jeanne adopted four older children—two siblings from two different families—when they were both in their 50s, and Jeanne quit her teaching job to keep the new family going. Sally Alice once again became a grandma, providing those four children with additional love and support. Bob and Jeanne helped Sally Alice to organize her move to the retirement community and to clean out her house, and also sprang her from a very unsatisfactory rehabilitation center after a fall. They have been an integral part of the effort to keep the Center for Peace and Justice from financial failure. Jeanne comes to Sally Alice's apartment to empty the garbage and do the laundry several times a week, and they continue to have Sunday dinners and celebrations together.

Chapter 5

Human progress is neither automatic nor inevitable... Every step toward the goal of justice requires sacrifice, suffering, and struggle, the tireless exertions and passionate concern of dedicated individuals.

Dr. Martin Luther King, Jr., pastor and civil rights leader

Sally Alice Thompson had been born Alice Hollcroft, but it wasn't until the early 1980s that she changed her name. She had never liked the name Alice, and Sally felt less drab and ordinary. This name change came at a time when her life also took a dramatic new turn as she launched herself onto the international peace scene, giving herself new confidence and direction. It all began with the Great Peace March of 1986—a valiant national effort to eliminate nuclear weapons.

The atomic bomb used in WWII and created at Los Alamos National Lab in New Mexico opened a whole new era in global warfare. After it was dropped on Hiroshima and Nagasaki, to the dismay of some of the scientists who created it, the world woke up to the power of this new technology and its capacity for destruction. About 140,000 people died in Hiroshima on August 6, 1945, and another 75,000 several days later in Nagasaki when a second bomb was dropped. Untold thousands suffered horrible deaths from radiation poisoning and cancers for years following the initial explosions.

The very first resolution of the newly created United Nations General Assembly in 1946 was aimed at curbing the production of nuclear weapons. However, the victors in the war, the US, Britain and the USSR, were not ready to listen. The military/industrial complex, recognized and named by General Dwight Eisenhower, was already blazing into existence, greedy for the opportunity for growth and profit. Giving in to the corporate push of the weapons industry, governments began to frame the debate in different terms, using the word deterrence or "mutually assured destruction" (MAD). In other words, no state will be the first to use weapons that can annihilate the planet, if that means they will be destroyed along with it.

By the 1960s, people had lived with the threat of a nuclear apocalypse for more than a decade. Americans were sick and tired of the Cold War with the USSR and the huge expense and insanity of building a stockpile that could destroy the planet. Covering one's head while hiding under a school desk seemed like a ridiculous idea to teach kids in case of a nuclear attack, but many people of my generation remember doing just that. The peace movement built momentum through groups such as the Federation of American Scientists, Women Strike for Peace and the Student Peace Union, calling for test ban treaties and non-proliferation treaties. An A-bomb test in the Bikini Islands in 1954 that irradiated the crew of a Japanese fishing boat, and the Cuban Missile Crisis that brought Soviet missiles within miles of US shores in 1961, heightened awareness of the grave dangers of nukes. Linus Pauling, a bio-chemist and peace activist, won the Nobel Prize for Peace in 1962, adding to the message of the insanity of continuing to build nuclear weapons. This brought some success with a limited test ban treaty, and a non-proliferation treaty with the USSR in the 1960s.

By the 1980s, when the election of President Ronald Reagan brought the acceleration of the arms race, the movement had grown and was becoming impatient. In 1982, nearly a million people descended on New York City to protest the proliferation of nuclear weapons, joined by other mass protests in Europe and Japan. Following on the heels of that was the Great Peace March of 1986, planned by David Mixner, a veteran of protest against the Vietnam War and an activist during the early days of the HIV/

AIDS crisis. He was also founder of Pro Peace, People Reaching Out for Peace, and he used the non-profit status of Pro Peace to raise funds for the march. Mixner had hopes of 5,000 participants marching across the country demanding the total elimination of nuclear weapons. According to his early calculations, he would need $20 million to pay for 2,500 tents; 1,275,000 showers; 20,000 pairs of shoes; and 3,825,000 meals, as well as trucks, permits and other equipment.

When Sally Alice heard of this march, she was intrigued and, after some thought and discussion with Don, she decided to join. It would be a wonderful extension of her peace work, she thought. Don said he couldn't think of anything more boring, but he would support her by showing up now and then. Sally Alice said Don liked to plan ahead, keeping a "card catalog" of things he'd like to do and see in the future. With her sense of adventure, she liked to be spontaneous and take risks. She headed for Los Angeles and joined 2,000 other committed women, men, and children. Holly Near sent them off, inspired by her song "One Step for Peace," among others. Marchers walked the 114 miles from LA to Barstow, a small city in the California desert, pitched their tents and awaited further instructions from Mixner, who was to arrive with supplies and money to pay for the rental of trucks and equipment. As revealed in the introduction, he arrived by helicopter only to tell people to go home, the march was out of money. His initial goal of raising $20 million had not been met, and his staff hadn't been paid for three months.

It's hard to imagine the chaos, disappointment, and anger at that point. Nevertheless, 800 people refused to give up, among them Sally Alice. Various reasons motivated them to stay: trying to get the attention of Washington DC, talking one-to-one with people across the US, searching for a sense of personal meaning, and acting on religious principles.

Judith Rane, an elderly friend of Sally Alice's and a fellow marcher, added her own perspective to the story when I interviewed her in Taos. She'd heard about the march on the radio in Canada and came down from Vancouver where she was a systems analyst for the first generation of personal computers. She'd walked in a peace march in 1976 organized by the War Resisters League. After the initial shock and disappointment of Pro Peace's bankruptcy, small groups of marchers organized in an effort to save the march, and some of them became the leaders. There was agreement that initial organizing efforts by Pro Peace had been top-heavy and authoritarian, so now organization came from the grassroots, where decisions were based on consensus. Judith must have come off in all the chaos as someone calm and pragmatic, because she ended up as one of a board of eight directors. They immediately went into lockdown, hid all the rented vehicles, and delegated responsibility to those with ideas. Some of the rentals were renegotiated and others were returned. Once word got out that this had turned into a grassroots effort, donations began to pour in. They ended up with a refrigerated truck for the kitchen, a water truck, a school bus for a nursery school and a library, and a truck for porta-potties and showers. Early on, records were kept on a bank of computers until the generator broke down.

The march took off two weeks after reaching Barstow. This city in motion elected a mayor and was even assigned a zip code by the post office so marchers could get mail. (No cell phones in 1986.) The board worked with pro bono attorneys to get the necessary permits and plan the logistics of the route and the stops along the way.

Sally Alice quickly saw the need for more transportation and fundraising supplies, so Don delivered their small sedan, named by marchers The White Dove. She began to design buttons, T-shirts, and bumper stickers to sell at each stop, and the White Dove quickly became too small to accommodate it all. She then bought a van and shelves were installed along the sides for storage. Finally, her efforts outgrew the van as well, and she paid for a school bus that became her studio and shop. Through the years of their employment, Don and Sally Alice had invested in rentals in Albuquerque that helped them save money. They both agreed that the needs of the march and other social justice causes were excellent reasons for spending much of that money.

As the march progressed, Sally Alice made elegant postcards to sell from black and white photos of people and places on the march. Judith pointed out that Sally Alice never asked what she could do—she saw it and did it, as she'd always done. "She was quiet with a loud scream of accomplishment—a secret warrior, a diplomat in disguise with a kind smile, a steady hand and an eye always on the goal," Judith said. "You hardly noticed her until you suddenly heard of all she had done." Sally Alice set up tables at every stop and was responsible for 90% of the funding that came in donations of $25 or less. Robert Redford and a few others donated as much as $25,000, and Joan Kroc, the wife of Ray Kroc, founder of McDonald's, donated Caldecott books, children's books that had won the sought-after Caldecott medal because of their beautiful illustrations and content. Their sales went to funding the march as well.

Another perspective on the march came from Melinda Williams, who was 11 at the time and marched with her grandmother from Nebraska to Washington DC. Melinda is middle-aged now, happily married to a pastor. She was thrilled to share her stories of the march one hot afternoon in Albuquerque, where she is helping her mother run two residences for disabled and elderly people. Her grandmother, Lee Simms, raised four grandchildren after the death of their mother, Melinda's aunt. Lee had been a social justice activist all her life. As Melinda said, she was born holding a picket sign. Lee started out with her eight-year-old granddaughter, Mia, youngest of the four she was raising, who walked with her to Lincoln, Nebraska, hating every minute of it. Melinda could hardly wait to take the place of her cousin. She thought it was the most exciting thing she'd ever done, and those memories can still bring her to tears. By the time she joined, Lee and Sally Alice were close friends. Melinda has a photo of them, lying together in a tent with cold towels on their legs and their feet sticking out of ice packs. The march created a lifelong friendship among the three of them. After the march, Lee even moved to Albuquerque and became a familiar face at the Peace Center and at Sally Alice's dinner table. Melinda said conversation was always about current events and justice issues of the day.

Melinda wanted to experience everything on the march, and because

Sally Alice allowed her to handle the money sometimes, she enjoyed hanging out at the fundraising table that Sally Alice erected at each stop. As always, Sally Alice didn't have a megaphone to attract attention to herself, but Melinda remembers her talking earnestly and passionately about the cause to those who stopped by. Sick children were allowed to ride in the fundraising bus, and once, when Melinda had poison ivy, Sally Alice brought her a stuffed monkey, Oreo cookies, and Hershey's Kisses. She remembers the marcher/clown who could juggle on a unicycle and also how she and the other children were fascinated, in spite of the horrible smell, when Portapotty Bob allowed them to help with pumping out the potties. Being a night owl, Melinda would stay up to watch the practice of the marchers' band, Collective Vision. They played a wake-up song each morning which, until just recently, Melinda kept as the ringtone on her phone.

Sally Alice always asked Melinda what she had learned at the end of each day, and 37 years later, Melinda still remembers a lot about those lessons. One indelible memory was seeing a place where slaves on the Underground Railroad sometimes waited days until it was safe to travel to the next sanctuary—a windowless room so small that people couldn't even lie down. Another was the eternal flame the marchers carried from coast to coast, as well as the street theater on August 6 to commemorate the dropping of the atomic bomb on Hiroshima and Nagasaki. To Melinda, a mixed-race child of 11, these were unforgettable and "very emotional" vignettes of American history.

Before Melinda arrived, Sally Alice, Lee and granddaughter Mia, Judith, and the other marchers had first walked into Arizona and then up through Las Vegas. Sixty-five miles north of Las Vegas, a couple hundred marchers planned a protest at the Nevada Test Site, and 80 chose to be arrested in an act of civil disobedience. Their action delayed a planned test by only two days, however. They were detained in jail for two weeks, but eventually caught up with the others still walking. In St. George, Utah, they met with people in denial that the above-ground testing of nukes in the deserts of the Southwest from the 1950s through the 1970s could have caused an increase in the number of cancers, especially among young people. Sally Alice, who knew a lot about the effects of fallout because of the testing of the bomb in southern New Mexico, urged these "downwinders" to think about the possible link, although by then the Limited Nuclear Test Ban Treaty of 1982 had forced testing underground. By 1990 the Downwinders Act (Radiation Exposure Compensation Act) was passed by Congress and awarded people suffering from certain cancers such as thyroid and leukemia with some monetary compensation, but this act recognized only some of those impacted. Nearly 40 years later, this is an ongoing issue as the Downwinders Act expires in 2024. Victims and activists believe it must be renewed and broadened to include families near the Trinity test site and Native uranium miners who were left out of the original act. The film, "Oppenheimer," released in the summer of 2023, has brought national attention to the issue as millions of Americans witness the dramatic story of the building and testing of the bomb in New Mexico. Sadly, any mention of the people impacted by the Trinity test, or the uranium miners, was left out of the film.

In Nebraska, marchers ran into farmers who were bitter and resentful as they watched agribusiness shut down their small farms and towns while the government did little to help. Spirits got trampled by the heat, humidity, and hostility there, but in Iowa whole towns turned out to welcome them with picnics, potlucks, and pony rides for the kids. One town was even able to find homes for each of the marchers for a night. In Wellman, Iowa, Sally Alice contacted a woman she'd attended high school with, and they spent an afternoon together. They had become friends because both had considered themselves outcasts. The woman's husband took them around to see the houses they used to live in, but not one of them was still standing. This shocked Sally Alice, but helped her realize just how dilapidated they must have been. Her friend was still an Iowa girl who hadn't seen much of the world and wasn't political. The two women didn't have much in common except their past, but Sally Alice was glad she'd made the contact and hoped she left them something to think about.

On August 6, marchers commemorated the 41st anniversary of the devastating bombing of Hiroshima by cutting out shadow figures of people doing activities of normal life to represent the shadows on the walls of the city after the bomb was dropped. These shadows were left when the bomb exploded and the intense heat and UV rays changed the color of walls and buildings. If someone had been in front of the wall, a shadow was left behind

Marching through the Midwest

before the person was incinerated. This was the street drama that left such a lasting impression on Melinda. Judith was also immensely moved by it. She'd been focused on herself and her struggle to quit smoking for months before, she said, but after that memorial action, she never touched another cigarette. Other more current events added to the power of the marchers' message that summer—the radiation leak at a nuclear power plant in Chernobyl, Ukraine; the bombing of Libya which killed and wounded civilians; and the failure of peace talks between US President Ronald Reagan and Soviet leader Mikhail Gorbachev.

The march continued for eight months through the rest of the United States, with marchers spreading their message of disarmament and peace to people in cafes and bars, parks, schools, and churches. In Davenport, Iowa, they ran into a Soviet/American peace group that had traveled 2,000 miles through the US. One beaming Russian woman, boarding a riverboat down the Mississippi, said, "We understand each other without words." That meeting may have planted the seed for the march through the Soviet Union a year later. Marchers also floated lanterns down the Mississippi, each lit by the Hiroshima flame they had carried all the way from California.

When the march reached Denver, Sally Alice could barely see out of one eye. She consulted an ophthalmologist and was immediately scheduled for a repair of previous cataract surgery. She called Don, who showed up as quickly as possible after the surgery to drive her to meet the march, which had gone on ahead. His speedy arrival underscored how he understood and appreciated the importance of the march to her. Within a couple days, she was back marching. When I asked her about the usual follow up appointments after surgery, she said, "I didn't think about that. All I cared about was that I could see and I could join the march again." That eye gave her no more problems.

Sally Alice remembers a woman who shouted "Read your Bible, you creeps!" along the way. Later, a pastor who had prepared a message about the power of Christianity realized, once he'd met with a group of marchers, that they had a lot to teach him too, and he listened. In Chicago, protesters lined the streets they walked along, shouting, "Socialists!" and "Get a job!" but in Cleveland they joined 5,000 people for the annual city peace march.

It wasn't all work and walking. There was a lot of talent among the marchers, and some wrote songs they performed at campsites as well as in public places as they marched. They sang and danced with Pete Seeger during a private concert at Red Rocks, Colorado, where Melinda got to try out his fiddle. Later, in New York, Yoko Ono tearfully hugged each marcher and said, "I love you," but Melinda didn't understand until later who she was and why it was such an honor. Jesse Jackson encouraged them in Chicago, and they had dharma time with Ram Das, who said, "When the human heart speaks out of deep truth of the absurdity, imbalance and fear of our culture, it resonates like a pebble dropping into the ocean." Their message went national when they were interviewed on the Phil Donahue show in Chicago.

There is a film on YouTube called the "Great Peace March of 1986," produced by marcher Catherine Zeutlin. It's well-made and inspiring, highlighting the patience, problem-solving, and perseverance of the marchers, as well as the fun and connection the march created. I wish it had more than 600+ views. I've watched it several times to write this section, and each time I tear up at the beauty and sincerity of the faces, the idealism of the young folks, and the weary wisdom of the older folks, all so hopeful that the march would make an impact on America and the world. The tremendous determination and dedication present, sometimes in the face of great hardship, is poignant. You see marchers jumping across stones to avoid the water and mud in their campsite after a rain, persisting in the face of negativity and protest, and triumphantly getting across the Rockies. Imagine sleeping on the ground for more than eight months at the age of 65 or bringing an eight-year-old along to walk 15 miles a day! Courage and conviction showed up every day. Love and joy showed up, too. The marchers planted trees in each town they passed through, and Melinda remembers digging the hole for the Malcolm X memorial tree in Omaha, Nebraska, his birthplace. Now she would like to retrace the route of the march to see how big the trees have grown. There were six weddings along the way and one 50th anniversary celebration as well as one death from a car accident, a tragedy that hit the marchers very hard. In Omaha, Don arrived again for the Fourth of July festivities and read "The New Colossus," by Emma Lazarus, part of which is now at the base of the Statue of Liberty. It was his favorite poem and he shared it often. Here are a few lines most people may never have heard because the others are so famous:

> Here at our sea-washed, sunset gates shall stand
> A mighty woman with a torch, whose flame
> Is the imprisoned lightning, and her name
> Mother of Exiles.

After walking 3,700 miles, the march finally made it to Washington DC on November 5, 1986, where it was greeted by 15,000 people lining the route. One of them was Don, there to celebrate Sally Alice's amazing achievement. The march's ranks had swelled back up to 1,200 by that time. There was a feeling of triumph in the air but also of sadness as marchers contemplated leaving those that had become like family through months of shared purpose. Many of them linked arms, sweeping across a park and singing in a round:

> Dear friend, let me tell you how I feel.
> You have given me such treasures,
> I love you so.

Tears fell like the autumn leaves around them, but smiles always broke through as marchers embraced in long bear hugs. Comments like, "This march turned working for peace from an activity into a lifestyle," and "I will never be the same after this" were heard everywhere as they said goodbye. The Reagan administration never acknowledged the march, but several marchers managed to meet with the National Security Council. Sally Alice felt that the power of what they did lay in the one-to-one contact and conversations they'd had along the way, planting seeds in people's minds and leaving behind the trees at each stop as reminders. Perhaps its greatest public recognition came from being nominated for the Nobel Prize for Peace in 1987.

Chapter 6

At any given moment, we have two choices: to step forward into growth or to step back into safety

Abraham Maslowe, psychologist

The story of the Great Peace March does not end here, however. Allan Affeldt, a young marcher at the time, got to thinking about jibes encountered along the march such as, "Take your message to the Soviet Union!" Why not? he thought. He immediately began talking to others about organizing such a march in the USSR, but when he approached the Soviet embassy, he was told Americans could not walk through the USSR. Franklin Folsom, a member of the board with a lifetime of socialist activism behind him at the age of 78, would not take no for an answer. He flew to Moscow and met with the Soviet Peace Committee, discovering that they had watched the US march with great interest and were enthusiastic about helping to plan one there. Alan then arranged for visas, recruited volunteers, and worked out logistical details.

The march began in the spring of 1987. Sally Alice set out along with Judith Rane and Frank Fulsom as part of a group of 200 Americans and 200 citizens of the USSR. They were all there to show that the people of the two world superpowers wanted to live in peace and bring an end to the Cold War.

The marchers were treated like astronauts, according to Sally Alice.

They traveled by train to Leningrad, where the march began. Smiling women came out to offer trays of bread and salt, symbols of welcome, as marchers walked by their homes. During the 439 miles from Leningrad to Moscow, they leapfrogged every two days between riding a bus and walking. Two Russians and two Americans shared a tent each night. In Moscow, Alan helped to arrange a huge concert to celebrate the Fourth of July. As Judith commented, "The people of the USSR desperately wanted disarmament and so did we. When two countries are ready to consider peace, people-to-people encounters are very effective."

This is how Sally Alice found herself marching to Moscow one day in step with a handsome young man from Turkmenistan. His name was Murad Nazarov, an English teacher at the time and later Turkmenistan's ambassador to India. She'd barely heard of Turkmenistan and had never heard of its capital city, Ashkabat, the home of her marching partner, but they started chatting about their lives. His English was good, and he told her of his city, located in a dry desert surrounded by mountains, where many people wove and made jewelry for a living. Ashgabat had a university and a rich culture of art and music. "My goodness", Sally Alice thought, "it sounds so much like Albuquerque!" They quickly agreed that Albuquerque and Ashgabat should create a relationship as official sister cities. But they weren't sure how to go about that.

The peace march ended for Sally Alice with the news that Del had taken his own life in North Dakota. She desperately tried to get back to be with Don, but she was too far away. Del had already been buried in the Santa Fe National Cemetery when she finally made it home. Overwhelmed with grief, she and Don both felt that healing would come only from continuing their work.

Chapter 7

Activism is the best cure for depression that I know.

Yvon Chouibrand, founder of Patagonia

Healing for Sally Alice began with the journey to formalize the sister city relationship between Albuquerque and Ashgabat. This entailed a lot of communication with Turkmenistan, which was a very slow process in those pre-Internet days. Letters between the two cities could take weeks to arrive. Government officials of both cities had to find accord during at a time when the US and USSR were still in the midst of a cold war. At a hearing in front of Albuquerque's city council, one teacher testified against the idea, saying, "I've been teaching my students that communism is bad and that these people are our enemy! How can we do this now?" Finally, however, Sally Alice's perseverance and the encouragement of many friends paid off, and the two cities became sisters when both mayors signed the Sister Cities Protocol on July 25, 1990.

Even before the agreement was signed, Sally Alice had decided that she wanted to get to know this place so similar to her own city, and yet half-way around the world. She arrived in Ashgabat, after first landing in Istanbul and Moscow and changing planes, "in a trance of jetlag and wonder," as she describes in her book *Central Asia Fantasia: Transitions in Turkmenistan, A Spiritual Journey,* self-published in 1999. It was 1990 and Turkmenistan was still a part of the USSR. The dismal prospect of two weeks of making her way with no language or contacts had worried her before her arrival, but her worries were soon put to rest. The Turkmen people had been unable to travel or welcome most foreigners for years under Soviet rule, so everyone wanted to meet an American. Hospitality is key to Muslim cultures, and Sally Alice was treated to several lunches and a dinner party each day she was there. A holdover from nomadic days is the saying, "The guest is higher than the father." She received gifts wherever she went. She was never allowed to help in the kitchen, no matter how many times she visited; the hot water heater was lit whenever she arrived; and her hosts even helped her take off her shoes at the door and put them back on when she left. "The inveterate klutz," she writes, "was embarrassed by all the attention, but she liked it a lot!"

Turkmenistan is a tiny country in Central Asia inhabited mainly by the Turkmen tribe and surrounded by other "stans," including Kazakhstan and Uzbekistan. "Stan" means "place of" in Persian. All of these Central Asian countries endured centuries of invasions, the Arabs bringing Islam in the 8th century and the Mongols carrying out bloody incursions into the 1400s. Thousands were killed, but Central Asian cities also provided oases on the Silk Road for hundreds of years until the advent of the railroad. Caravans of silk, spices, and tea also brought with them the exchange of goods and ideas. The city of Merv in Turkmenistan became a center of literature and the arts, but was burned to the ground in a Mongol incursion. The mix of cultures through trade and war created a renaissance of discoveries in mathematics and astronomy, and a flourishing of the arts and architecture while Europe limped through the Dark Ages.

During the 1800s, Russia and Britain vied for power and influence in this region in what is called The Great Game. Both were intent upon increasing their empires, and especially claiming India. Central Asia was on the way to India, and much of the Great Game played out in this region. Ultimately, Russia prevailed in the "stans," while India became a British colony. After the Bolshevik Revolution of 1918, Central Asia became part of the Soviet Union, and places where tribes, nomads, and traders lived were carved up into Soviet republics under the rule of the USSR. To make sure no republic became too homogeneous and unified, Stalin forced people from different ethnic groups to move to different republics. For example, some people from Azerbaijan were forced to move to Kyrgyzstan and begin new lives there, where they became second class citizens as more Russians moved in. Life in the "stans" was hard and repressive in many ways, but under the Soviets, people at least had the security of food and homes, humble as they were.

When Sally Alice first arrived in Turkmenistan, glasnost was beginning to bring changes to the USSR, and thus to the Central Asian countries. Mikhail Gorbachev was loosening the grip of communism; allowing elections with multiple candidates; giving more freedom of speech to the press and the people, including criticism of the government; and allowing the public practice of religion once again. Sally Alice was delighted to be hosted by both Christian priests and a Muslim imam. Churches were opening, and although people practiced Islam mostly in their homes, the first mosque in Ashgabat had recently opened. Businesses were preparing for less economic control.

By the time of her next visit, banners lined the streets announcing a successful referendum that had created a Turkmenistan independent of the USSR. In fact, there was no more USSR, and these newly independent countries were cut loose to fend for themselves. Imagine, after being so tightly controlled for over 60 years in every aspect of life, what this meant to these tiny countries! I have not been to Turkmenistan, but while traveling in Kyrgyzstan and Uzbekistan, we heard the stories of those years of transition between total dependence and independence. People who had had basic needs covered on a daily basis suddenly had to fend for themselves to find staple foods, housing, and jobs. The economic system had to be recreated. Instead of being part of a giant system, each country had to find an independent means to support itself. It was chaos for a long time, and many older people we spoke with looked back to the security of the Soviet system with nostalgia. Now they were forced to sell family heirlooms, carpets, and jewelry just to survive. Many of the leaders under the Soviet regime went on to become leaders under independence, but, having been trained by the Soviets, governments continued to be repressive. Among them, Turkmenistan's was one of the worst, and still is today.

While the many hardships and history Sally Alice witnessed over the years play a role in *Central Asia Fantasia*, the people of Turkmenistan won her heart, and she returned there again and again to experience their warmth, hospitality, generosity, and grace in the face of a harsh life. Tatiana Vetrinskaya, another of Sally Alice's "daughters," stands out because of the close friendship that continues to this day. Sally Alice loves opera and classical music, and this enthusiasm inspired her Turkmen friends to give a concert in her honor during each of her visits. The combination of Western classical music and the haunting traditional Turkmen music moved her, and she greatly admired the accomplished musicians. After one such concert, a lovely young pianist approached and, in halting English, offered her phone number. Intrigued, Sally Alice called the next day and was invited to the pianist's apartment for dinner, where she also met her husband, Sasha. They became fast friends in spite of the language gap. Sally Alice learned that Tatiana (Tanya for short) had seen Sally Alice on each of her visits, and, determined to get to know her, had been studying English. Their friendship provided the practice Tanya needed to improve very quickly.

Tanya's story reflects the hard work and determination of many people Sally Alice encountered and grew to love in Turkmenistan. She was born after the great earthquake of 1941, which killed her brother and drove her parents to Latvia. Her musical talent was recognized early, so she attended Russian schools of music as a youngster. When she was 10, her father died of a heart attack and her mother moved back to Ashgabat to care for her own bedridden mother. Within a few years, she, too, became an invalid, and teenage Tanya took on responsibility for the care of both mother and grandmother while continuing her study of music.

When Sally Alice first met Tanya, she was living in a one room apartment with the love of her life, Sasha, who helped care for her mother. The apartment contained two couch/beds, a wardrobe, and a piano, and had a tiny kitchen and even tinier bathroom. Like all Turkmen women, Tanya invited Sally Alice and other friends over often, and cooked lavish meals for them.

One time Sally Alice invited Tanya and Sasha and a few other friends to try an American dinner. It took her days to find all the ingredients for spaghetti, salad, and brownies in the markets of Ashkabat. She had brought the chocolate from the US, but could only find a huge, four-liter jar of tomato sauce. She prepared the meal and was awaiting her guests when there was a knock on the door. One of the guests she'd invited stood there alone, pointing to her coat. Finally, Sally Alice understood that she was supposed to go with him. He took her to Tanya's house, where Tanya had prepared dinner and their other friends were awaiting her. They had a good laugh over the miscommunication and enjoyed Sally Alice's American meal the next evening.

The conditions of the lives of the women of Turkmenistan were difficult at that time. There was little processed food, so everything was cooked from scratch, even noodles. Supplies of ingredients could be hit or miss. Some homes had running water, some even had hot water, but others had an unpredictable supply that could be full of sediment. They had to heat water for laundry on the stove, scrub clothes in the bathtub, and hang clean laundry on a line outside the apartment. In Sally Alice's apartment at one time, the water came on three times a day so she could turn on the *kolanka*, the water heater in her bathroom. However, the water pressure sometimes went so low that the *kolanka* could blow up, so she couldn't leave the bathroom as it heated up. She couldn't take a shower when there was so little water pressure either.

Women took great pride in their appearance and wouldn't leave home without every hair in place, nails done, and clothing immaculate and crisply ironed. Most walked to a bus stop to get to work after walking their children to school, and buses were crowded, forcing many to stand in the aisles. They repeated these trips at the end of the day.

Even with these demands on her time, Tanya persisted with her musical study and became a very accomplished pianist. Sally Alice encouraged her to apply for a scholarship to University of New Mexico, but she needed to be enrolled to apply. Tanya came to the US fully expecting to receive the scholarship and begin her graduate studies in music. All who knew her talent were stunned when the scholarship was awarded to someone else, leaving her to fend for herself in a foreign land. Fortunately, she had Sally Alice and Don. Tanya lived with them for eight months while teaching piano lessons, pet-sitting, and picking up accompaniment gigs around town to stay afloat. She managed to get by and to save enough money to bring her beloved Sasha to the US. Today, she is the highly successful owner of the New Mexico School of Music, offering lessons on a variety of instruments to hundreds of young people taught many teachers. Sally Alice and Don helped the young couple by lending them money to start the school and to buy their first home.

All in all, Sally Alice made 29 trips to Turkmenistan between 1989 and 2014, when she turned 92. She writes with great affection in *Central Asia Fantasia* about the many women and families she became close to, some of whom visited the US. In addition to making these beloved friends, she was involved in student exchanges with high school students; mayoral exchanges between the two cities; and a grand cultural exchange of musicians, dancers, athletes, and poets between Ashgabat and Albuquerque. Imagine making the long, 36-hour trip packed into a small seat on an international flight at the age of 90, and then add the work of organizing and attending these events as well.

Sally Alice closes her book on Turkmenistan with these words: "I have high hopes for my adopted country. [I hope that] increasing democracy, increasing citizen participation [will] bring about a beautiful atmosphere where the remnants of foreign occupation will be forgotten, where the wonderful characteristics of the Turkmen people and their neighbors will bloom with new life and vigor." She adds about her own experience there, "I have been given so much in return for the time and money I have expended in my Central Asia efforts. The knowledge I have gained, the wonderful friends, the great adventures... The realization that life is definitely not over when one has retired. Being the recipient of the openhearted acceptance of such loving people, I have been truly blessed. The ugly duckling has finally emerged as a swan!"

Chapter 8

I'm no longer accepting the things I cannot change.
I'm changing the things I cannot accept.

Angela Davis, civil rights activist and professor

Trips to Turkmenistan, beginning just a year after Del's death, helped Sally Alice heal the raw wound of losing him. The warmth of the Turkmen people was the medicine she needed. But there was plenty going on for her and Don in New Mexico as well, and they continued to find purpose in their projects. In the early 1980s, Sally Alice had been one of the earliest members of the Albuquerque Center for Peace and Justice (APC&J), supporting its creators Dorie Bunting, Kent Zook, and Blanche Fitzgerald. Robin Seydel, a volunteer in the early years, said that the original founders established a loving and nurturing environment. For example, Robin lived with Dorie for a while, and Dorie returned all her rent payments when Robin decided to buy a house. Robin described Sally Alice as a get-it-done kind of woman with a good sense of humor, skilled at providing options, solutions, and conflict resolution that helped move discussions forward. In those early days, they held Ban the Bomb Cafes with bands and food, supported the women's movement at its zenith, and raised money for Central American refugees in sanctuary in California. Sally Alice showed up at almost every event.

Originally located in a small office run by volunteers, the first two paid staff came on board in the late 1990s, when the thriving Center moved to a larger building that previously had been the Albuquerque Bahai Center in the University District. The Bahai Center wanted to sell to a group working for world peace, but the ACP&J needed money to make that purchase happen. Many fundraising events took place, and ultimately, Sally Alice and Don agreed to sign for the $157,000 mortgage to get things rolling. The ACP&J made monthly payments to the Thompsons. Robin Seydel and Judith Kidd, another volunteer, were hired as co-directors. When Don died in 2010, Sally Alice paid off the remainder of the mortgage with cash. At a party attended by dozens of members, she burned the mortgage papers. Today, she admits that she couldn't find the actual papers, and burned an empty sheet of paper instead. But it did the trick, and the ACP&J was free of debt.

Over the years it blossomed into a network of more than 70 non-profits that fell within the arc of peace and justice: nuclear weapons and accountability of New Mexico's national laboratories, racism, indigenous issues, environmental concerns, and reproductive rights. These groups made up PAJOLA, Peace and Justice Organizations Linking Arms. The Center published the best newsletter and calendar for keeping up with events in town and opened welcoming arms to those needing a place to belong, a place to make a difference. During COVID-19, however, difficulties emerged that led to financial struggles and almost resulted in the Peace Center being dissolved. Many, many dedicated members and volunteers stepped forward to resolve financial problems and get the organization back on its feet. There are still obstacles ahead, but folks continue to pull together to resolve each hurdle. It looks today like the Peace Center has a promising future and will be around to support concerned community members in their efforts to address issues of social and ecological justice for years to come.

Don's path took him to the state legislature, where he served four years in the House and four years in the Senate, beginning in 1975. They were some of the most fulfilling of his life. He was progressive and collaborative, tackling issues like Open Space designation, the Equal Rights amendment, funding for quality education, and assistance with day care expenses for working mothers. New Mexico's legislature meets for only 30 days one year and 60 days the next, when budget takes precedence over all other matters. Legislators are unpaid. It's an intense and often thankless job, but Don loved it. He was devastated when he was gerrymandered out of his district by "the Good Ole Boys" network, which didn't agree with his other progressive goals such as raising taxes on oil and gas production, not taxing social security benefits, and reform of the criminal justice system. Many of these issues still plague New Mexico today. After leaving the legislature, Don took over management of the rentals he and Sally Alice had bought. He also worked on the Social Concerns committee of their UU church and joined the Friendly Philosophers Club, where he sometimes presented on such subjects as the Constitutional aspects of censorship. Always a swimmer, he won medals in the State Senior Olympics, and most proudly, a bronze medal at the National Senior Olympics in 1999 in St. Louis.

Sally Alice and Don continued to live in their big house together with their huge Great Dane, Puccini, named for the love they both had for opera. They had adopted Puccini after he jumped into the open window of their car at the post office one day when he was a small puppy. They were both dog lovers. and had no doubt that he had chosen them to be his forever family. Full grown, he came up to Sally Alice's hips. Visitors were terrified that he would knock one of them over with his affectionate energy, but miraculously that never happened.

Age catches up with all of us eventually, along with life's inevitable transitions. Don died in 2010 after a long and debilitating illness. Sally Alice believes that after he was gerrymandered out of the legislature and Del died, he lost his strong sense of purpose and slowly went downhill. Don was in and out of the hospital and rehab frequently in his final years, but he always came home to be cared for by her. As it became difficult for him to walk, Sally Alice took him by car through southern Utah, visiting Bryce Canyon and Arches National Parks, and giving him a last spectacular encounter with America's beauty. Although she was in her late 80s, she did all the planning, driving, and necessary caregiving along the way. She was steadfast, as she had been throughout their 61-year marriage. A young friend came to help at night, and eventually Don went on hospice; otherwise, Sally Alice was by his side. As he grew more fragile, friends came to help walk Puccini, who returned the favor with grateful face licking. Don maintained a sense of humor, claiming that walking around the long dining room table counted as physical therapy, and he usually had a grin and even a joke for visitors despite his obvious physical discomfort. After his death from heart failure, Sally Alice did what she'd always done in the face of grief—she kept going, always aware of the needs of the community and other people.

Chapter 9

The secret of change is to focus all of your energy not on fighting the old but on building the new.

Socrates

With the loss of her life partner, Sally Alice was alone in her house, this time permanently. It was too empty and too quiet, and she and Don had always offered their home to friends and travelers when needed. Working through immigrant rights groups, she decided to invite refugees from Central America and Africa, whom she welcomed despite language barriers. New Mexico at the time had the only detention center for trans women fleeing abuse and death in religiously conservative countries all over the world. It was 75 miles from Albuquerque, and when detainees were released, she often provided a place for them to feel safe before heading out into the world to meet their sponsors. She'd never been very involved in LGBTQ+ issues, having lived most of her life before they were talked about much, but her compassionate heart understood the loneliness and isolation of these women and their need for safety. She'd been there herself.

Saliou, an asylee from Guinea, West Africa, lived with her for a minimal rent payment and helped her with yard and housework. After two years, he was one of the last to leave when she decided she had to move.

Saliou still honors her with a visit during the festival at the end of Rama-
dan. As the house became more of a burden, Sally Alice asked me to take
her to see Brookdale, the retirement community where a friend lived. We
took a tour and she liked it, but the needs of refugees and trans women
continued to keep her at home.

Without Don to care for, she was free to travel again, and upon hearing
that Roger and I were organizing a trip to Cuba in 2015, she told us that
she'd always wanted to go. We jumped at the chance to travel with Sally
Alice. She immediately made her own arrangements, and at the age of 92,
awaited us with a grin in the international terminal in Mexico City a few
weeks later. During this time, President Obama had opened up travel for
Americans to Cuba if they were going for "cultural/educational explora-
tion." Fidel Castro had retired from his powerful leadership role that had
lasted from the end of the Cuban revolution in 1959 until 2008. He'd
replaced himself with his brother Raul, who opened Cuba to a different
model of tourism. In Havana and Trinidad, we slept in *casas particulares*,
the homes of Cubans who had the money to transform a room in their
home into a rental for tourists, usually providing breakfast as well.

Our group of eight travelers was dispersed to *casas* in a residential neighborhood of Havana, meeting after breakfast for the day's activities. Sally
Alice was ready to go every morning, keeping up easily with a group at least
25 years younger. When she stumbled coming down the stairs at the *casa*
in the World Heritage city of Trinidad one day, her host refused to let her
out alone again on the cobblestone streets of the city. We returned after a
morning walk to find her fuming with indignation at her detention, and
highly insulted to have been singled out because of her age. With typical
Sally Alice spirit, she enthusiastically participated in every event, including
riding along the ocean on the Malecon in a blue 1955 Chevy and flinging
herself across the hood for a photo. When we were having our last drink
on the last night, she commented, "I really enjoyed traveling with all of
you. Not an asshole in the bunch!"

Chapter 10

Aging is not lost youth; it is a new opportunity for strength and growth.

Betty Friedan, feminist

For several more years, Sally Alice adapted in order to continue living in her home. After urging from friends, which she had angrily and stubbornly resisted, she stopped driving. Two one-car accidents finally convinced her that they were right; but, of course, this was life-changing. Her calendar was still filled with events every day, but now she had to arrange for transport, too. She bought a three-wheeled, open-air vehicle she could stand in to operate, but by that time she didn't feel stable enough to drive it alone. Saliou enjoyed driving it around the neighborhood, though. She was dependent on others to get her around, and her multigenerational community came through for her. More meetings were held at her house, and usually someone was willing to help her get where she needed to go.

Finally, however, she admitted that it was time to leave her home for a simpler way of life. It was evident that she was no longer safe in a house that was falling apart around her. She was tired of cooking, climbing her circular metal stairs to open the solar tromb window every morning, trying to keep up with repairs, and even having so many people around all the time. The final decision to move to Brookdale wasn't easy, but her friends supported her, and many folks joined in to make it happen. One day Mandy and I met with her in her bedroom to help sort out her personal things, especially her hundreds of T-shirts with logos ranging over decades of causes: Earth Day, Nicaragua, Veterans for Peace, Ban the Bomb, Dennis Kucinich, Sister Cities, Raging Grannies. She chose a dozen special ones to keep and wear, and we decided to make the rest available as mementos of Sally Alice for those attending a celebration to honor her and the 35th anniversary of the Peace Center a few weeks later. When Sally Alice suggested she throw her large earring collection all into one bag, Mandy was horrified by the vision of untangling all those earrings, so we also spent some of that afternoon putting them into different boxes to keep them safe. Her Turkmen "daughter" Tanya stopped by and tried to convince her to leave her battered folding chairs behind, but she insisted that she needed at least 10 places to sit in her new apartment. She was sure that she would continue to host many meetings after her move. Jeanne Pahls and Bob Anderson and their children helped pack up the house and move her things into her new, third floor apartment.

Once she got to Brookdale, her apartment buzzed with people helping to set up the Wifi, arrange lighting, hang art on the walls, and stock kitchen supplies. In this flurry of activity Sally Alice insisted that she wanted to keep her new home "spare," not cluttered like her old house had become. The only things she brought to hang and display were Sarita's watercolors, art done by her great-granddaughter, Savana, and photographs of loved ones. She left many framed awards behind.

A few days after the move, she commented that waking up in a new place wasn't as hard as she'd anticipated. She loved being able to just show up for a meal, and as time went by, her kitchen filled up with vases of dried-up bouquets and eventually her walker. She never touched the stove, and the fridge contained just a few cups of ice cream, her favorite treat brought from the dining room. The coffee pot was the only thing that ever got used in that new kitchen.

Several weeks later I stopped by to visit and found a Sally Alice I hadn't yet known—an elegantly dressed woman in black doing a crossword puzzle with her feet on the coffee table. As usual, dishes of candy sat on the table and vases of flowers and an orchid surrounded her, housewarming gifts from her many fans. The south-facing window was full of bright geraniums blooming in the sunlight. The bed was neatly covered with a bright spread, and all was tidy. I asked her if she was happy in her new home and she replied, "I'm not sure I would say happy, but I am content."

Those beat up folding chairs that Sally Alice insisted on taking to Brookdale continued to be well-used as she carried on with her organizing work. One of her favorite causes continues to be Veterans For Peace (VFP). She and Don had created the Don and Sally Alice Thompson Chapter in 1988, and members continued to meet in her apartment to strategize.

Sally Alice with Mandy and Charles

Veterans For Peace was created in 1985 by 10 veterans in response to the endless arms race and, especially, US intervention in Central America. Today, this organization has 120 chapters located in every US state and in Vietnam, the United Kingdom, Japan, and Ireland. It also holds a permanent seat in the United Nations as a non-governmental organization and is a member of the International Peace Bureau in Geneva, Switzerland. Since its inception, VFP's goal has been to create a culture of peace by sharing the experience of military veterans. According to their website, their work includes: "educating the public, advocating for a dismantling of the war economy, providing services that assist veterans and victims of war, and most significantly, working to end all wars." They work at the intersection of racism, inequality, and the environment in their efforts toward peace.

The Albuquerque chapter is located in one of the most militarized, nuclearized states in the country. VFP members demonstrate outside Kirtland Air Force base, lobby against the focus on nuclear weapons at Los Alamos National Laboratory (LANL), and provide tables of information at most community events. In 2020, they were to host the VFP national convention in Albuquerque, scheduled for the commemoration of the 75th anniversary of the dropping of the two atomic bombs on Japan on August 6, 1945. Because LANL was created to build and test those bombs, recognition of the event in Los Alamos was obvious. At the age of 96, Sally Alice was a key organizer, finding the venue and working with the chapter to plan the schedule. The convention was canceled in person in 2020 due to the beginning of COVID-19, but it was replaced by a dynamic Zoom presentation covering speakers and workshops. Unfortunately, the money pouring into New Mexico from the national labs and the military make lobbying against them very difficult, partly because New Mexico is such a poor state and partly because the military/industrial/congressional complex has become so well-established. It is hard to get the attention of state or national legislators on these issues, but VFP refuses to be discouraged, continuing to hold vigils in Los Alamos.

One of the goals of the Albuquerque chapter has been to get the city to change the name of Veterans Day, November 11, back to its original name, Armistice Day. They feel this name better recognizes the original intention of the day to honor the end of the "war to end all wars," World War I. The original Congressional legislation read, "it shall be a day dedicated to the cause of world peace and to be hereafter celebrated and known as Armistice Day." In a published editorial to the *Albuquerque Journal* by VFP members Charles Powell and Kris Hardy, the chapter invited people to join chapter members in ringing a large bell 11 times "at the 11th hour of the 11th day of the 11th month." This, the letter said, would honor the sacrifice of veterans and civilian victims of war, as well as emphasize a commitment to peace. In 2018 state, county, and city government officials issued a proclamation in honor of the centennial of that first Armistice Day, thanks to the work of the Albuquerque VFP Chapter.

In 2015, the VFP national convention was held in San Diego, where

Roger and I were living a little north of the city to help my elderly parents. Sally Alice stayed with us that week, catching a ride downtown at 7 am and returning about 10 pm after meetings and workshops ended. She was the oldest attending member and was honored for her work during the convention. Her endurance was remarkable—according to her, she was the only one who danced aboard the harbor tour one evening. Roger and I attended several days of the convention and were impressed and motivated by the speakers, including retired Colonel Ann Wright, one of three members of the state department who resigned in protest when Iraq was invaded; journalist Seymour Hersch; author Phyllis Bennis; and other inspiring activists and veterans of Korea, Vietnam, and the Middle East. As VFP members say, "If you want to thank me for my service, work for peace." They purposely keep the F in VFP a capital letter to emphasize that they work FOR peace.

Before the convention that year, a VFP crew had nearly finished restoring a sailboat called the Golden Rule at a Humboldt County shipyard in northern California. This boat had belonged to the Quakers, and in the 1950s, it was outfitted to sail from California to Hawaii and then to the Marshall Islands in hopes of stopping the above-ground nuclear testing the US was doing there. The tests of the US and the USSR had put so much radiation into the atmosphere that it was appearing in cows' and mothers' milk in many places around the world. Sadly, the boat never completed the entire mission—it was boarded twice by the Coast Guard and once it got to Hawaii, the crew were arrested. Happily, though, the mission and its failure, along with other worldwide campaigns, helped bring attention to the issue, resulting in the Limited Nuclear Test Ban Treaty of 1963.

The boat was sold in 1958, and its whereabouts became a mystery. It wasn't seen again until 2010, when it appeared badly damaged in Humboldt Bay. A few members of VFP in that area decided to restore the boat and use it to continue its mission to educate the public about the dangers of nuclear war. Members with knowledge of sailboats came to pitch in from all over the country. The boat generated a lot of excitement when it sailed down to make an appearance at the San Diego VFP convention, but it wasn't quite ready to present to the public.

Two years later, Sally Alice called and asked Roger and me to help her realize a dream. She wanted to make the Pacific Ocean the final resting place for Don's ashes. She'd waited eight years, and the Golden Rule was finally seaworthy. She successfully made all the arrangements, and one summer morning we headed out on San Diego Bay aboard the Golden Rule with a group of veteran sailors. San Diego County is a heavily militarized area, and we joked as we made our way out to sea that the helicopters and military jets flying constantly overhead were an honor guard for Don. Sally Alice had Don's ashes in a Greek urn and we brought a bouquet of roses. A film crew from Australia just happened to be aboard and interviewed Sally Alice for a film they were making about the boat. As the bay opened into the ocean, she leaned over the side and quietly poured Don's ashes into the water. We dropped roses into the gentle wake of the boat and read a Rumi poem. For her this was a last tribute to the love and dreams of a 61-year marriage. For us it was a great honor to be present. Today the Golden Rule has renewed its mission and has traveled around the South Pacific and through US waterways, providing education on nuclear topics and peace-making.

VFP continues to be an inspiration and source of meaning for Sally Alice. Its website and newsletter provide trusted information in these times of "fake news" and Internet overload. Humble as she is, Sally Alice does not boast of her peace-making efforts or financial contributions, but a friend who attended the 2019 VFP national convention heard from others "in-the-know" that Sally Alice had recently made a very large donation to the organization. She has never mentioned this to her friends in Albuquerque.

Chapter 11

The right song at the right moment can change history.

Pete Seeger, singer and song writer

Another group bringing inspiration, meaning, and friendship to Sally Alice has been the Raging Grannies. This feisty group of older women sing songs pointing to the issues of the day, using well-known, sing-along tunes, and perform them at protests and as street theater.   They dress in long skirts and big floppy hats, belying their sharp wit and courage. Some have participated in protests for decades, while others are new to the idea of standing up for what they believe. The Raging Grannies began in British Columbia, where a group of older women was outraged by the arrival of nuke-bearing American ships anchored in the harbor off Vancouver. No one in Canada seemed aware of what was going on, so they created songs to wake people up and performed them around the city. Now there are gaggles of Grannies throughout Canada and the US, sharing lyrics and posting their songs on YouTube.

Grannies have been raging in Albuquerque since the 1980s, when several mothers of the Center for Peace and Justice decided to create a local group. Sally Alice even took guitar lessons at the age of 80 to accompany them. At that time, they were a "youngish" old, in their 60s and in their prime. Now Sally Alice is the last of the original Grannies, but youngish others have replaced them. I, myself, am now a Raging Granny, and I love these spirited women who drop everything to show up at a demonstration, farmers market, or peace activity. Sometimes we're on the program and sometimes we stand and sing as people arrive. We pass out copies of the lyrics and always are joined by grinning younger people urging us on. It's a joy to be a Granny.

Having loved word play and rhymes since childhood, Sally Alice has written many of the lyrics, and now she's been joined by a talented fellow writer, Marcy Matasick, who also plays guitar for the group. In 2021, in the midst of the pandemic, we opened the program for a Support Roe v. Wade demonstration in Santa Fe.

Sally Alice with a newspaper photo of the original Grannies

COVID made gathering risky, especially for older folks, but the Grannies turned out on a lovely fall day and were greeted by a small but appreciative crowd of women of all ages and some men. Uteruses and fallopian tubes made of papier-mache floated through the crowd, and many T-shirts read "Don't Snitch on Our Snatches." This T-shirt was an answer to a new, draconian Texas law that encouraged community members to alert authorities about any Texan looking to get an abortion after a fetal heartbeat was heard. The Grannies opened the program, and the young faces up at the front of the crowd reflected the energy we created as things got going. When I arrived at the rally that day, Sally Alice was sitting on her walker holding a sign that read, "He who hath no uterus must shut the fucketh up. Fallopians 21:2."

Here's a sample of what we sang that day to the tune of Battle Hymn of the Republic:

Never Turning Back

Battle Hymn of Women

They want to take us back

To when the only rights were men's

They want to choose how many kids we have and even when,

And what we wear from burkas to bikinis, just for them

These edicts we condemn!

Rise up, women! Join together!

Solidarity forever!

We shall not retreat—not ever,

For women's time has come.

Later that day there was a similar rally in Albuquerque, and Sally Alice wanted to be at the Veterans For Peace table. We hurried from the Santa Fe rally and made it to the Albuquerque rally with an hour to go before it ended. We parked on the street quite a long way from the entrance of the park, and I got her walker out of the car. Sally Alice looked around and saw the low berm lining the sidewalk along the park. She said, "Let's go over this thing because I've got to see Charles at the VFP table." I looked at it dubiously but figured she knew her capabilities and limitations. After watching her sit on the berm and swing her long legs and long skirt over onto the grass, I saw that getting up from there was going to be challenging. But I placed the walker in front of her, gave her a boost from below and, miraculously, after several attempts, she heaved herself up. With nary a moment to pause and catch her breath, she set out, pushing her walker across the grass. Walking alongside her was like marching in a parade with the beauty queen—people all around us were waving, calling her name, and trying to get her attention. She smiled and waved back serenely. Finally, I went home, leaving her at the VFP table to get a ride home with Charles at 5 pm after leaving that morning at 9. She was 97.

In October of 2022, Sally Alice turned 99. She wanted to wait till she turned 100 to have another party (the year before she'd had five different parties), but the Grannies had a different idea. Sunday morning we all showed up at the Peace Center at the beginning of the UU Fellowship

service dressed in our long skirts and bonnets, and surprised her with some of her favorite songs, as well as one composed just for her to the tune of "It's a Wonderful World."

The Raging Grannies sing for Sally Alice's birthday

Here are the words, written by lyricist Marcy Matasick:

She's Our Sally Alice

She has marched for peace—worn out her shoes,
from coast to coast across Russia, too
She's our Sally Alice
She inspires us all.
Took in immigrants and refugees,
Knowing that all deserve equality,
She's our Sally Alice,
She inspires us all.
A lyricist and writer, a singer in the streets
From serving in the Navy, to Veterans for Peace,
She has traveled the world, and wherever she goes,
Kindness and grace are what she sows.
Though the world's a mess, so much despair,
she keeps on striving to make it more fair.
She's our Sally Alice
She inspires us all.

NEVER TURNING BACK

I could barely sing through my tears as she beamed up at us from her walker. After more stories and songs, we broke for a potluck that included her favorite chocolate tres leches cake and Mermaid Sparkle ice cream. Here's a sample of the songs for some of the other issues the Grannies support.

Stop the Frack, Jack! (to the tune of *Hit the Road, Jack***)**
Mother Nature is angry, she's got the shakes
That's why we're having so many earthquakes.
Time to stop the assault, so much is at stake
Gotta save our planet for our grandchidlren's sake!
Stop the frack, Jack
And don't you come back no more no more no more no more.
Stop the frack, Jack
And don't you come back no more.

Big Oil vs. Life on Earth (to the tune of the Marine Hymn)
From the sand dunes down in south Iraq
To the wild Alaskan seas,
We have trashed the earth to pump the oil
Just to fuel our SUVs.
We have overthrown democracies,
To exploit their oil reserves
Intervened in sovereign nation-states
Cause it's Big Oil that we serve.

Our Vision (to the tune of Battle Hymn of the Republic)
Mine eyes have seen the glory
Of a coming world of peace
With the blessed end of poverty

Never Turning Back

Equality's increase
Where there's no such thing as
Weapons of mass murder factories
A world that's safe and free.

(See other Raging Granny songs in the Appendix on pg. 83.)

Chapter 12

You are never too old to dream a new dream or set a new goal.

Audrey Hepburn, actor

In 2010, the US Supreme Court made a controversial ruling in a complicated case called Citizens United vs. Federal Elections Committee. The ruling allowed that corporations have "personhood" and money is a form of free speech. This meant that corporate donations to political campaigns are protected by the First Amendment. In his dissent, Justice Stevens wrote, ". . . corporations have no consciences, no beliefs, no feelings, no thoughts, no desires. Corporations help structure and facilitate the activities of human beings, to be sure, and their "personhood" often serves as a useful legal fiction. But they are not themselves members of 'We the People' by whom and for whom our Constitution was established."

But the 5-4 decision became the law of the land. Since then, corporations and wealthy mega-donors have been able to make huge dollar donations to groups called SuperPacs, which sprang up to get around the provision in the ruling that donations could not be made directly to candidates or their campaigns. The influence of "dark money," meaning contributions that can't be traced to a source, became more common and larger. This ruling helped to create the most expensive election in history up to that point between Barack Obama and Mitt Romney.

This infuriated Sally Alice because it gave more influence to the wealthy and served to make the voice of the people less powerful in a country where financial inequality becomes worse every year. Candidates, even at the state and local level, need more and more money to run for an office, limiting opportunities for working people and people of color to launch a campaign. Sally Alice was fed up (and maybe also a little bored). She hadn't walked across anything big for almost thirty years, so she hatched a plan to walk to Santa Fe, 60 miles from Albuquerque, carrying a mop with a sign that read MOP, Money Out of Politics. She outfitted her car for sleeping and eating, got herself some good walking shoes, and contacted her podiatrist, who showed up twice along the way.

The occasion began with a press conference where, unfortunately, the reporter misunderstood her cause and reported it as her wanting to reduce government spending. Undeterred, she set out accompanied by a small group of friends who helped with her car. The road paralleled the freeway between Albuquerque and Santa Fe, a quiet road that ran through fields of alfafa and cattle. When that road ended, she drove across to the east side of the Sandia Mountains and continued up a back road that meandered through small towns of the high country, climbing about 1,000 feet. Not once did she have to sleep in her car—people came out of their homes with offers of food and lodging along the way each day, and some joined the march for short distances. Sally Alice arrived in Santa Fe 10 days after she began, having made at least a few people along rural New Mexico highways more aware of our money-driven election system. As usual, even one person being better informed made the effort worthwhile for her—and it had been another grand adventure. A crowd greeted her when she reached Santa Fe, and they shared a triumphant lunch with state Senator Dede Feldman on the steps of the capitol building.

Chapter 13

A bend in the road is not the end of the road—unless you fail to make the turn.

Helen Keller, educator for the blind and deaf

Throughout her life, Sally Alice has continued to stay informed about and involved with events in Central America, using School of the Americas Watch and Veterans For Peace to find information. In her opinion, mainstream media don't provide truthful coverage of US efforts to defend corporate economic interests rather than support democratically elected leaders in the region. During the 1980s, she lived in Nicaragua for short periods. Nicaragua at that time was struggling in multiple ways: the cruel 44-year dictatorship of the wealthy Somoza family; the efforts of the socialist FSLN, or Sandanistas, to oust the Somozas; and the efforts of the US trained and backed Contras to defeat the Sandanistas, including the mining of the harbor of Coriento that was condemned by the World Court. On top of that, throughout the 1980s and 1990s, earthquakes killed as many as 10,000 people and hurricanes killed and left homeless tens of thousands more, devastating the country.

Many Americans were acutely aware of this and spent months in Nicaragua building homes, providing health care, and helping farmers. Teachers in the US collected books to send to devastated areas. Sally Alice showed up five different times, living with families or in schools, sometimes sleeping on shelves. Once, she helped build a school in the north and another time, she picked coffee in the south. She says she witnessed atrocities perpetrated by the Contras such as the bodies of Sandanista supporters dismembered and thrown into a well. She met Daniel Ortega, leader of the Sandanistas, and his cabinet and, to this day, she remains loyal to Ortega and what he has accomplished for Nicaragua, including a national health system and free public education.

Similar events occurred in other Central American countries, and Sally Alice was in Guatemala and El Salvador as a witness at crucial times. According to her, Hillary Clinton, Secretary of State under President Barack Obama, continued the policy of "sending planes with armed personnel to Honduras and Haiti to kidnap democratically elected presidents in order to protect US economic interests." Civil war, coups, political corruption, US meddling in elections, gang violence, and violence against women and children continue to plague the region with little discussion of responsibility, or human rights assistance from the US. Thousands of people have been forced to flee and now wait at our southern border, hoping for safety and a future for their children. Back in 1991, when glasnost brought an end to the Iron Curtain and the cold war, Sally Alice wrote a published letter to the *Albuquerque Journal*, expressing her sadness at the way the plight of Central American countries is ignored in the US:

> What a wonderful moment in history: The people of the Soviet Union triumph over the power of the army, the secret police and the forces of repression!
>
> And what a remarkable occurrence: The official sympathy and support of the United States is with the people. And what a profound tragedy that we continue to condone, justify and financially support the tyrannical, repressive forces in Central America! If only we could recognize the deep longing of the people of El Salvador, Guatemala, and yes, of Nicaragua, for their share in the freedoms and human rights to which all of God's people are entitled, we would have learned a priceless lesson from the fearsome events of the past few days.

Moving to Brookdale simplified Sally Alice's life, but it also gave her more time to think about what's important and what she could still do. Contentment was not something she'd ever valued much. As we sat in her apartment one day, looking through an album of family photos, she quietly mentioned that she was going to start a fast against US sanctions and sieges. "Try to be at the UU fellowship tomorrow," she added. "I'm going to give a talk about what our government has been doing and has done in Central America."

Next thing we knew, she had announced the fast, which she called FASS, Fast Against Sieges and Sanctions, at the UU service that Sunday and had begun to fast that very day. Emails flew through the activist community. People tried to convince her that her activist work was more valuable than sacrificing her health, and possibly her life, in such a gesture. Many were wondering without voicing it whether Sally Alice had decided to make her

A young supporter greets Sally Alice at a protest against sanctions and sieges

death meaningful in this way. She'd moved out of her house, sold most of her belongings, and decided that the money from the sale of her house would go to the Center for Peace and Justice.

I stopped by the next evening, Day 2 of the fast, to try to understand what her intentions were. Sally Alice had long been horrified by sanctions against countries our government opposed. These sanctions starved women and children by preventing basic humanitarian aid from getting to civilian populations. The people suffered, not those in power. Roger and I had met Sally Alice protesting sanctions against Iraq in the

1990s. People starved, but it took an invasion to bring down Saddam Hussein. Other sanctioned countries over the years have included Venezuela, Nicaragua, and Cuba. Recently ships have sat in the harbor of Yemen, pre-

A TV reporter interviews Sally Alice about her fast

vented from unloading life-saving supplies by a US-backed coalition involved in Yemen's civil war. I suggested that the administration in Washington was not going to change its policy because of a one-woman fast in New Mexico. Sally-Alice replied, "People don't know the truth about what the US is doing around the world. A well-educated friend of mine thinks sanctions are a kind of tariff! If I can raise the awareness of two or three people, it will be worthwhile. And I'm hoping others will join me in the fast, at least partially."

As usual, she was adamant. She'd made up her mind and would be announcing it at the regular Tuesday rally of RESIST near the offices of Congressional representatives and senators. Again emails and calls flew through the activist community: Be there on Tuesday to support Sally Alice!

On Tuesday, Day 3 of her fast, about 75 people arrived carrying signs: Love Not Hate Makes America Great; No War, No Sanctions Against Venezuela; Love Persists, Love Resists. The Raging Grannies sang. A columnist from the *Albuquerque Journal*, Joline Gutierrez Krueger, showed up unsure about how to present Sally Alice's latest endeavor. She recently had written about the 35th anniversary celebration of the Center for Peace and Justice and Sally Alice's award that night. Now she didn't want to encourage that same woman to endanger herself with this fast. But Sally Alice had said that spreading the word and asking people to join her fast was one of her goals. Joline knew from a single interview that Sally Alice is one determined woman.

Sally Alice sat on her walker to make her statement to the press, and she read it with difficulty in the bright light. She said:

This is the third day of Fasting Against Sanctions and Sieges (FASS). I am fasting because I empathize with the many hungry children of the world, so I am joining them in their suffering. I am outraged that our country is engaging in sanctions and sieges that result in starvation of babies and children. I am profoundly saddened that my government interferes in the affairs of other countries, refusing to acknowledge that sovereignty and to respect their dignity. . .

I am almost 96 years old. The short remainder of my life in inconsequential. . . those children have a right to live!

Permitting our country to continue down this road of genocide is completely unacceptable. So I have decided that, instead of asking, "Why doesn't somebody do something," I looked in the mirror and said, "You're somebody. Do something."

I invite anyone who shares these feelings to join me in my fast, by skipping a meal or fasting for a day or longer. I would like to know of anyone who joins me. Please contact me at this email. I hope this can start a movement to eliminate sanctions and sieges. Please help me: demand that we lift all sanctions and cease all sieges!

After her announcement, a reporter interviewed her on camera for a local TV station. She appeared on the news that evening. Nearly every day for the next week I went to Sally Alice's apartment, half expecting to find her in a robe on her bed looking exhausted. But every time, she was fully dressed and buzzing with excitement. Often there were two or three people in the bedroom, working to get her online so she could receive the many emails of encouragement and solidarity in her apartment instead of down in the lobby. She asked a friend to help her find an efficient way of recording each one, and she announced the totals each day to her visitors. Conversation was often interrupted by incoming phone calls from friends and the media. She continued to attend every event she had scheduled that week, as well as interviews with reporters, radio stations, and online news sources. She was thrilled with the response.

Thursday afternoon, however, she commented that she was feeling pretty unfocused and couldn't concentrate on reading the paper. It was the first time she'd mentioned any consequences of the fast aside from being hungry, but Friday she was back to composing her next press release. On Day 7, she released the following statement:

So far I have received 121 emails, phone calls and Facebook messages, 38% of which are from folks who are joining me in the fast. I don't know where all the messages originated . . .but the most touching messages came from two South Koreans who thanked me for working to lift the sanctions from North Korea. I was very gratified by one of the emails I received from a person I don't know named Judy Warnock: "Your fast has come to my attention, and I want to let you know that it has made a difference to me. I guess I had not thought about all the children in the context that you are, but you have definitely made this come to light for me. Thank you for you dedication to this important cause."

This is a step toward the goal of FASS: to bring to the awareness of Americans the tragedy that is done in their names. When enough people become aware of the atrocities that are occurring, we will no longer tolerate them.

I urge everyone to urge their congresspeople to work to lift the sanctions and end the sieges. All are invited to join in also by fasting in whatever manner they find is appropriate for them. This might be a total fast or skipping a meal. In this way we can empathize and experience to a certain degree the suffering of the children who are starving. Please let me know if you are joining the fast.

Saturday morning, Day 8, I received an email from a fellow Raging Granny. It said, "I just talked to Sally Alice and she's changing the way she's doing the fast. She will skip lunch but go back to eating breakfast and dinner." Attached to the email was a photo of FDR and the song "Happy Days Are Here Again" by Ben Selvin and the Crooners. It captured the feelings of all of us perfectly. By modifying her fast, she would remain healthy to continue doing her important work—not that she had ever really stopped. For months, she skipped lunch and ate only two meals a day in the spirit of keeping the fast, and herself, alive.

Chapter 14

It does not matter how slowly you go as long as you don't stop.

Confucius, Ancient Chinese philosopher

It is now June of 2023. We have survived the COVID-19 pandemic that brought many changes to our country and the world. And to Sally Alice as well. She received an electric wheelchair from Medicare that allows her to travel around Brookdale easily, and when she goes out, she uses a walker. She rid herself of hearing aids that never did the job well, and has adopted a listening device that she points at the speaker. She is frustrated that it works well when a few people are present but not so well in large settings. She spends more time on her couch, Zoom, and the phone than in face-to-face meetings, and some days she says "everything hurts." Yet her mind is still sharp, and she stays well-informed about the issues she cares about. She tries not to miss an Amy Goodman episode of "Democracy Now!" or investigative journalist David Barsamian's "Alternative Radio" with speakers like Noam Chomsky and Naomi Klein. Recently she told the story of her activist life to fellow residents at Brookdale and received a standing ovation. She still attends the lay-led, humanist UU fellowship she started in the 1980s.

A few months ago, she gave a presentation to that small congregation about conditions in Central America, where she made so many visits. Whenever there is a Raging Grannies opportunity, she'll show up, sit throughout on her walker, and be the last to leave, no matter the weather. Recently I was about to leave a protest because of a frigid wind, until I saw Sally Alice still sitting on a berm wrapped in a long overcoat, listening intently. I sheepishly changed my mind. When Roger and I stop by to visit,

Sally Alice waves to a car parade around Brookdale for her 97th birthday during COVID-19

she still eagerly engages in the affectionate insults and teasing that she and Roger love.

On March 10, 2019, a year before the pandemic locked down whole nations, the Albuquerque Center for Peace and Justice celebrated its 35th anniversary and honored the work of Sally Alice in a festive occasion at the African American Performing Arts Center. An invited speaker was again retired Army Reserve Colonel Ann Wright, a 29-year Army veteran and diplomat to several Middle Eastern countries. That night she spoke of Sally Alice's participation in the peace march in the US and USSR and said, "She's got a heart of gold and feet of Teflon." Jim Harvey, director of the Center for Peace and Justice, commented, "You represent all that is right and all that is good." Someone else called her "the conscience of Albuquerque," and her granddaughter-in-law said, "She makes me feel so young but not because she's old. Because she constantly reminds me of what's right and important as a younger person." Later, the city of Albuquerque declared Sally Alice Thompson Day on February 5, 2021. Mayor Tim Keller presented the award for her work and generosity, locally, nationally, and internationally.

NEVER TURNING BACK

Sally Alice turns 100 this year, in October 2023, after more than 70 years of efforts to make the world a more just and peaceful place. Last week in her apartment, we discussed the state of our world today: Russia's invasion of Ukraine and the ongoing war there; the serious and unsolved immigrant crisis at our border; climate crises that worsen year by year; a nuclear laboratory in New Mexico that will produce triggers for a new generation of nuclear weapons; a Peace Center recovering from a crisis. I asked her what her advice to young activists would be right now. After a long, thoughtful pause, she sighed and replied, "Don't give up. We just can't give up. We have to continue putting one foot in front of the other, learning and speaking the truth, and working together. I am inspired by those articulate young people I see demonstrating in front of the base and around town. We need their leadership and they need our support."

When asked about the meaning of life at the age of nearly 100, Sally Alice said that a life well-lived is a life full of meaning and purpose. And, she added, "The search for meaning gives us purpose." Sally Alice has found meaning around the world, from the small towns of the Midwest to Moscow, from Albuquerque to Ashkabat, and from small gatherings in her living room. Never have these efforts been about self-aggrandizement or even appreciation. She does it because she has to in order to live with herself, to satisfy her innate sense of justice and to "pay the rent for living on this planet," as Alice Walker wrote. In doing so, she has brought meaning to her own life and an inspiring example to all those who know of her. Just today an article in *The Atlantic* from the September 2023 issue entitled "The Resilience Gap" showed up in my inbox. Resilience, the ability of individuals to overcome adversity and hardship, is crucial to a sense of well-being and personal agency. Author Jill Filipovic writes, ". . . social change becomes possible only if our movements are made up of people who believe that the adversities they have faced are surmountable, that injustice does not have to be permanent, that the world can change for the better, and that they have the ability to make that change." Those words fit the life of Sally Alice Thompson perfectly.

Appendix
Songs of the Raging Grannies

Weapons in Space

Tune: She'll Be Comin' Round the Mountain
Lyrics: Sally Alice Thompson

If you want to be the boss of this whole place
Then you've got to get some missiles up in space
You can cow the whole dang world
With your empire's flag unfurled,
and you're sure to launch a nuclear arms race

Now we've got a lot of armaments for sale
And they're going to bring in profits by the bale
Sell to Israel and Pakistan,
Ukraine, the Saudis, and Japan
And never send the profiteers to jail!

Oh, it's glory hallelujah and Amen!
A dandy, cool new arms race will begin
Put the burden on the backs
of the citizens we tax
And we'll really, yes we'll really rake it in!

Stop the Frack, Jack!
Tune: Hit the Road, Jack

Stop the frack, Jack
and don't ya pollute no more, no more, no more
Stop the frack, Jack, and don't ya pollute no more!

We want clean water coming out of our wells
but you poison our water so bad it can kill
You're turning this sacred place into a hell
so you better start packing and haul out your drills

Stop the frack, Jack
and don't ya pollute no more, no more, no more
Stop the frack, Jack, and don't ya pollute no more!

You're spewing out methane into the air
speeding up climate change everywhere
And you're spewing out benzene and silica dust,
Putting our infants and children at risk!

Stop the frack, Jack
and don't ya pollute no more, no more, no more
Stop the frack, Jack, and don't ya pollute no more!

Mother Nature is angry — she's got the shakes
That's why we're having so many earthquakes
Time to stop the assault — so much is at stake
Gotta save our planet for our grandchildren's sake!

Stop the frack, Jack
and don't ya pollute no more, no more, no more
Stop the frack, Jack, and don't ya pollute no more!
don't ya pollute no more
don't ya pollute no more

Stop Gun Violence
Tune: Darling Nelly Gray

Uvalde and Columbine, Las Vegas, Sandy Hook
Aurora, Parkland and Orlando, too
It's terrorism, fear and hate, the right wing likes to stoke
Legislators — What <u>are</u> you going to do ?!

"Thoughts and prayers" are how you stall
and get nothing done at all,
and your cowardice enables more attacks
You who sold your souls to the NRA, we're going to kick you out
We'll replace you with some reps who care to <u>act</u>

Australia used to suffer from atrocities like this
But they stopped it with some strong regulations
Now they haven't seen a massacre since 1996
Time for <u>us</u> to pass effective legislation!

Ban all weapons of war!
End the horror and the gore!
Keep all guns out of the hands of criminals
Ban the silencers and bump stocks. Mandate licensing of guns
Stop the terrorism of white nationals

What kind of a society would sacrifice their young
to exalt the rights of gun nuts and their guns?
We must honor human life, and the right to live in peace
We must value and protect our little ones
We say **never again**!

We're going to put an end
to the slaughter and the fear and the chaos
We are sick of always mourning for those cut down without warning
We're so tired of all this grief for loved ones lost

Spirit of Love
Tune: Home on the Range

The Spirit of Love
is encircling the earth
It is challenging hate, fear, and greed
It can bring to each person
the sense of their worth
It can bring us the peace that we need

Oh, our planet is small
It's our home, our provider, our mother!
We must make it a haven, a welcoming place
For every faith, every race

When we live together
like sisters and brothers
What a wonderful world this will be
The children can play
and the horses can run
and the butterflies flutter, safely

Oh, our planet is small
but it furnishes life to us all
We must make it a haven, a welcoming place
For every faith, every race

When we overcome our hate and our fear
and replace them with caring and trust
Then our cities will bloom,
field and forest will thrive
And the world will be peaceful and just

Ratify the ERA

Tune: Goodnight, Irene

A woman works longer and harder
in order to make a buck
Competence isn't a factor,
there's a ceiling and she's out of luck

Ratify the ERA! that is the way!
For equal work, it's equal pay
Ratify the ERA!

Women hold up half the heavens,
we should own half the earth
It's time that we be acknowledged
and paid for what we're worth

Ratify the ERA! that is the way!
For equal work, it's equal pay
Ratify the ERA!

Our foremothers mightily struggled
to get us the voting right
Now we continue to struggle;
for equality we have to fight!

Ratify the ERA! that is the way!
For equal work, it's equal pay
Ratify the ERA!

Safety for Women
Tune: Jesus Loves the Little Children

Every woman should be safe,
from brutality and rape,
safe from every form of cruelty by males
Every mother, sister, wife
has a right to peace in life
Men who don't respect that right should go to jail!

Sing for the safety of the women
all the women of the world!
Red, brown, yellow, black or white
must be safe by day and night
Let's eliminate the violence in the world!

Our Vision

Tune: Battle Hymn of the Republic
Lyrics: Sally Alice Thompson

Mine eyes have seen a vision of a coming world of peace
Where poverty is gone and threats of war forever cease
Where every child around the world is safe and loved and free
The world that's meant to be!

Glory, glory, jubilation!
We'll make peace with every nation
All the world is our relations
Our vision is the key

We reject the grapes of wrath, the bitter grapes of hate and fear
We see harmony with everyone, across the sea and here
And the day when Earth can heal from our abuse is coming near
Let's see this vision clear!

Glory, glory, jubilation!
We'll make peace with every nation
All the world is our relations
Our vision is the key

Medicare for All

Tune: On The Sunny Side of the Street

Grab your pen and sign your name
to a universal health plan!
Medicare For All:
Time to pass it, once and for all

We are here to tell you now,
to the nurses and the doctors
is where our funds should go
Not to greedy HMO's

Kick the insurers out
and save billions of bucks
Corporate "care" is a joke
No wonder we're so broke

'Cause the profits have no place
in the healing and the caring
Down with corporate greed
Single payer's what we need

So if we lose our jobs
we'll be covered still
We won't have big bills
to worry us, when we're ill

We'll see doctors of our choice
We'll really have a voice
Medicare For All:
Time to pass it, once and for all!

Immigrant Child

Tune: You Are My Sunshine

Back in my country, bad people chased us
And they scared my mama so
I saw her crying; they want to hurt us
And we knew that we had to go

We kept on walking, though I was tired
and I had blisters on my feet
We kept on walking when I was thirsty
And we walked when I wanted to eat

We kept on walking, when it was raining
We had to walk – no time to play
And when we got here, they handcuffed Mama!
Please don't take my mama away!

God Bless Our Planet Earth

Tune: God Bless America

God bless our Planet, Earth
world that we love
Let all creatures, and people
live in peace, like in heaven above
Bless the continents, and the islands
and the oceans, white with foam
God bless our Planet, Earth
our home, sweet home
God bless our planet, Earth
our home, sweet home!

Corporations Are Not People
Tune: Yankee Doodle

Corporations are not people; They have got no feelings
They can't laugh or shed a tear, they know not pain or healing
Corporations have no heart, they can't be empathic
Profit is their only goal — that's why they're psychopathic

Corporations are not people; they're a legal fiction
But the high Court said they are — Oh, what a contradiction!
Corporations are not men, They don't have erections
But the Court gave them the right to dominate elections!

Corporations do not eat, but they use lots of water!
Our economy they grabbed and took it to the slaughter
Corporations are not women, Never nursed a baby
But their bribes have rigged the game —
So they get all the gravy

Black Lives Matter
Tune: Bye Bye Blackbird

Freedom, justice for us all
That's our call, standing tall
Black lives matter!
Human rights for everyone,
Every daughter, every son
Black lives matter!

We condemn all race discrimination
It's an ugly stain upon our nation
We need safety in our homes,
where we shop, walk, or run
Black lives matter!

All the killing has to stop,
Prosecute killer cops
Black lives matter!
Fund the schools instead of jails;
help us thrive, win not fail
Black lives matter!

Put an end to mass incarceration
Now the people call for reparations
No one is expendable;
Everyone's valuable
Black lives matter!

Made in the USA
Monee, IL
10 October 2023